Gone Fishing…
…Fishing Gone

Gone Fishing…
…Fishing Gone

A memoir of a life at sea

Donald Turtle

Don Turtle

Published by Donald Turtle

ISBN 0 955 01060 8

Typeset in Adobe Caslon Professional

Designed and produced by WordMongers Ltd, Treen, Cornwall, UK
E-mail: turtle@wordmongers.demon.co.uk
Web: www.wordmongers.com

Printed and bound in Great Britain by Headland Printers, Penzance,
Cornwall, UK

Contents

Prologue

This book is both a brief autobiography of life at sea during World War II, and a record of the demise of one of our great natural assets, the commercial fishing industry, from one who has lived in it and taken an active part as a commercial long line fisherman for forty years.

On going through my father's belongings when he died, I discovered family Army medals belonging to relatives as far back as the British Raj and the Boer War. I now understand his surprise at my choosing the sea as a career, but I was delighted to be accepted at the Prince of Wales Merchant Naval School at Ingham, Norfolk in 1939.

Chapter 1

Starting my Sea Career

As the country was drawn into war, the early years of 1940–1941 saw the German U-boats rule the seas with impunity, surfacing in the middle of the convoy, choosing their targets, and after exhausting all their torpedoes, returning to port with victory pennants flying and the band playing through the town in a hero's welcome. The British merchant fleet suffered heavy casualties in both ships and seamen.

In 1941, on finishing my training, which gave me proficiency in communication, I found myself in South Shields signing on to the *SS Lagosian* as an Ordinary Seaman at the age of 16, with strict orders not to keep diaries or cameras. We loaded war materials alongside the quay and would await sailing orders to a destination known only to a few. One evening at dusk, just as I was going ashore to a cinema, the air-raid siren sounded, and within minutes six Stuka dive bombers, which were designed to make the most terrifying noise when diving, appeared from the clouds and proceeded to shoot down in flames all the barrage balloons in sight, just like a shooting gallery. They then picked their real targets – the gasworks. I had a perfect view and feared we might be next – when you hear a screaming plane, it is time to duck into any cover available, which I did. Fortunately it passed us, and a little later the 'all clear' sounded against fires and small explosions from the direction of the gas-works.

This little episode might have prompted the authorities to realize our vulnerability, for we soon received sailing orders, formed a convoy off Scotland and proceeded on passage to Freetown, West Africa, via the Western Atlantic, on a route that took much longer than normal to avoid U-boats.

The passage was one long routine of watch keeping, and as we sailed further south the bad weather eased to give calmer seas. As I came off watch late one evening a flash lit up the sky, followed by a dull boom. A four-masted merchant ship in the middle of the convoy had been hit by two torpedoes and was on fire. Ships were not allowed to stop, so we continued on our passage as the fire disappeared on the horizon. We later learned that the escort had picked up survivors.

We arrived in Freetown, discharged our cargo, then a number of natives called 'crew boys' boarded to do most of the work in return for their keep and a pittance. Our next port of call was Port Harcourt, further south on the coast, to load a part cargo of cocoa beans. We had to navigate some narrow waterways, with the jungle almost touching the ship's side. Listening to the screams and cries of wild animals and birds, we felt transported to another world. When we finally docked, an input and exit ramp was constructed over the ship's hold, and an endless stream of natives with hundredweight sacks of cocoa beans ran up the ramps, emptied their sacks into the open hold and ran down the exit ramp as one human conveyor belt. At the point of shedding their load, I noticed their bodies still retained the same bent shape, as if they had grown that way. For all this labour from morning until night they received 2 pennies per day, and had to be careful to avoid the police on the way home, on pain of being waylaid and relieved of their day's wages.

We loaded the remaining part of our cargo in the port of Lagos, then proceeded back to Freetown to discharge the crew boys and join the convoy back to the UK. I left Freetown, never to return, feeling a deep sense of injustice at the treatment of the natives.

The passage home proved uneventful, except that we were to rendezvous with another ship to join the convoy. When we reached the rendezvous point there was no sign of the ship, but a large area of flotsam floating where the ship should have been left no doubt as to its fate.

The remainder of the voyage saw no enemy action. Ships usually received their docking orders in the Western Approaches – ours was for the port of Hull. Since the Dover Straits were closed, as they were considered too dangerous, we had to steam along the west coast of England, around the north of Scotland, then south to reach our destination.

All the crew were paid off at the termination of the voyage, but the mate asked me if I would sign on for another trip. I thanked him, but declined the offer, as after five months away I wanted to see my family. Fate smiled on me at this point, as I discovered some years later.

All the main shipping ports carried a list of Merchant Seamen called 'the pool', administered on the same lines as an employment office. When my leave expired I was ordered to report to Salford Pool, the main port of the Manchester Ship Canal, where I joined a vessel called *Corner Brook*. The ship was named after a little shanty town in one of the inroads in the south of Newfoundland, which supported a paper mill. This was our permanent

A typical merchant ship, speed 10 knots, triple expansion steam engine. These liberty ships were mass-produced in America in as little as ten days.

Courtesy of the Imperial War Museum

destination. Sailing from Salford down the canal, I wondered why the Germans had never neutralized this waterway, which would only require the destruction of one of the main locks, leaving all the ships trapped in Salford Docks. I heard that there had been several failed attempts.

After leaving the last lock, we entered the River Mersey where the pilot boarded, taking us to the point of his station, which was the western part of Liverpool Bay. The route was littered with ship's masts protruding from the sea, the casualties of bombing.

After dropping the pilot, we formed convoy and proceeded into the Western Atlantic escorted by several destroyers and corvettes, which provided an outer protective circle. The passage usually took twelve days, depending on the weather, and during the winter we encountered the severest gales. I felt sympathy for the crews in the corvettes. Some, hardly bigger than a trawler, would roll in a calm sea. They must have had a terrible time, and it would have been impossible to prepare meals. After the torment of one bad weather crossing, they were likely to receive orders to turn about and escort another convoy on their return passage, and receive yet another plastering from the weather. But at least the enemy could hardly launch an attack in such weather conditions.

When the weather abated we would hear the occasional dull explosion of depth charges from the escort, which had made an Asdic contact, but I never saw any ships torpedoed on this outward passage. When the weather became calm it was usually near the Newfoundland Grand Banks, where we would strike another sort of menace – thick fog. Radar did not exist for merchant ships then. Imagine forty ships and their

A 'Flower' Class corvette

Courtesy of the Imperial War Museum

escorts suddenly engulfed in a thick bank of fog for several days. There were a few collisions.

Our first port of call was Halifax, Nova Scotia. We anchored in a basin near the docks to discharge sand ballast. The crew were given shore leave and most made for the drinking dens. I have been allergic to drink all my life – which is perhaps a blessing in disguise – so I headed for the Seamen's Rest to watch a movie. As I walked in there were notices pinned up asking everyone to be as quiet as possible, and especially not to slam doors, because many of the residents were torpedoed survivors suffering from shell shock. One such survivor was rescued three times from three different ships in just one crossing passage. I began to wonder what fate had in store for me.

We resumed our voyage north to Corner Brook and moored alongside the paper mill dock. I was surprised when going ashore to see that the place seemed to be full of beautiful girls, who were keen on taking us to the local dance – apparently most of the men were away serving in the Forces. One always remembers the first kiss: it happened to me there with a school teacher who was seven years my senior.

Loading the cargo of paper rolls took about a week. There was dancing every night, and all were loath to leave when it was time to depart. We left the port and some who had married there left with a heavy heart. When arriving in the open sea we formed a convoy and proceeded on our passage home.

The returning convoy was always loaded, and so offered more of a prize to the U-boats, which now began to hunt in 'wolf packs'. Several times during the return crossing it was necessary to make emergency turns to avoid interception. We reached the entrance to the Ship

An aerial view of an Atlantic convoy. 366,852 tons of Allied shipping were sunk in the Atlantic. If forced to make emergency turns in the dark without lights, shipping was faced with a worrying problem.

Courtesy of the Imperial War Museum

Canal safely and proceeded to Salford to unload our cargo.

I took my leave and then served another voyage in the same ship. For the second voyage we were made the 'Commodore ship' on the passage home. This meant that a high-ranking Naval officer and his staff boarded to direct the strategy of the convoy and communicate with the escorts from the ship's chart-room. This was separated from the wheelhouse only by a bulkhead. When it was my turn to steer the ship I could hear all the conversation between Naval staff and our escorts.

One evening I became attentive when I heard the dialogue becoming excited. It was a similar experience to listening to a running commentary on a fox-hunt. From the escort: 'Have sighted quarry on the surface.' 'I am going in for the kill.' 'Tally-ho!' Two minutes elapsed before the sky lit up. A deep boom, and then silence. The hunter had become the hunted. There was no news of any survivors.

We could hear the dull thud of distant depth charge attacks, but there were no other incidents. We arrived safely back to the canal entrance, and I signed off the ship.

I discovered that the requirements to sit the examination for a Deck Officer were four years 'sea time' in a deck capacity, and that the examination syllabus included astronomy, merchant ship stability, astral navigation, as well as levers of forces and communication (which I already had), so serious study was called for. I was determined to gain experience with different cargoes, so I joined the SS *Ocean Pilgrim* with war material for North Africa. This included heavy cargo like lorries which required specially rigged derricks. Merchant ships were

A destroyer steaming through heavy seas on escort duty

Courtesy of the Imperial War Museum

Typical anti-aircraft fire during a night raid

Courtesy of the Imperial War Museum

now fitted with steel-meshed torpedo nets, stabilized on the bottom corners with heavy lead sinkers. This saved my ship on the previous trip, when a torpedo hit the lead sinker and exploded outside the ship's hull, buckling the plates, which remained intact and kept the ship afloat.

The passage down to Gibraltar was uneventful, but ships always passed through the Straits of Gibraltar at night, away from the prying eyes of the German embassy, which was situated at a vantage point on the Spanish mainland.

We arrived at the French port of Arzew two days later and began discharging our cargo, which took another week. Following this we sailed down to Casablanca for phosphate and back north to Glasgow with no apparent enemy action. However, when the convoy was ordered to lift and stow torpedo nets, two of the ships on the outer edge of the convey discovered outrun torpedoes hanging in the nets. They were ordered to stand off while Naval personnel removed the torpedoes.

I signed off the *Ocean Pilgrim* in Glasgow and later joined the *Redgate*, a coal-burning tramp steamer. My first sight of her was when she was lying under a coal truck tip in the Manchester Canal, covered from stem to stern in coal dust from the railway trucks, which were up-ended to spill their contents into the ship's hold from a considerable height. When the ship was loaded and its hatches battened down it took quite some time to hose down and clear the waterways.

The pilot boarded and we proceeded down the canal into the River Mersey and joined the convoy bound for Naples. The convoy made a speed of 8 knots and experienced no enemy action throughout the two-week passage. We were ordered to dock at the port of Banoly near Naples, and were one of the first ships into Naples after the Germans left. When I stepped ashore I felt sickened and sorry to see some of the population – women with two or three little children covered in sores hanging on to their skirts and begging for food. One woman's life story was written on her face: husband killed and left to fend for herself.

The Italian dockers were discharging the cargo in lorries, which was going to take days, and every day the dockers would crowd around the mess door for the leftover food, which always resulted in an open pitched fight between them. Now and again there was an air raid, and as soon as the alarm sounded masses of people would run into the caves or shelters shouting 'alarmi', leaving the town wide open for looters.

Vesuvius was a good landmark for the German planes. One evening I was ashore with some of the crew and heard the familiar scream of a Stuka dive-bomber and ducked into a building. It was always an anxious moment when the screaming eased after the bomb was released. The raid lasted half an hour, and I fully expected to see the ship sunk, but the Germans had missed her.

The cabins on the ship were stacked with souvenirs, including firearms. The ship's firemen even had a Sten gun stowed in the corner of the stoke-hold to break up the very large lumps of coal. Discipline was lax everywhere. After Naples had received its allocation of coal, we were ordered to proceed to Sicily to discharge the remainder of the cargo. When we arrived in Sicily I became very ill, left the ship and was hospitalized for a couple of weeks.

After recovering, I made my way down the North African coast by train to Algeria, and eventually to Algiers, where I was housed in a camp with others to await passage home. One had to be careful of venturing into the town: the Kasbah was a labyrinth of narrow alleyways where you could feel a hundred eyes boring into you from behind the veils the Arabs wore. The rule was 'Never get caught in there after dark'. Those who did were often robbed, stripped or stabbed.

After three weeks we were all ordered to pack and be ready to leave the following day on a troop ship that was bound for Southampton. We boarded the ship as a mixed bag of passengers consisting of seamen, Army and Air Force personnel. There was no enemy action on the way home, and the Army organized some entertainment to break the monotony of the journey. We arrived safely in Southampton and I took some leave.

On reporting back to Salford Pool I was determined to gain some experience on bulk oil-carrying vessels such as tankers. I was lucky enough to be assigned to the *Commanche*, a tanker of the Anglo-American Oil Company, whose ships were all named after Red Indian tribes.

An outward-bound tanker in water ballast was one of the safest ships, as it was composed of numerous watertight compartments. If the ship were torpedoed, the ballast would absorb most of the shock and the water run out to sea level. During our outward-bound passage, I saw a Norwegian tanker in the next column receive three torpedo hits, which made hardly any difference to its flotation. I later saw the same ship moored in New York harbour, where it was awaiting dry dock with three huge holes in the side through which you could have driven a lorry.

On the other hand, a loaded homeward-bound tanker was one of the most dangerous vessels, and was usually

MT San Demetrio arriving in the Clyde after being torpedoed by U404 on March 17th 1942. At the time of being torpedoed, she had already been shelled by the German pocket battleship Admiral Scheer.

placed in the centre of the convoy to avoid the priority targeting of the U-boats.

The *Commanche* was mainly a lubrication oil carrying ship. 'Lube' has a fairly high flash point, so it was not as dangerous as tankers carrying high octane fuel with its low flash point.

We loaded our cargo of oil in New Jersey, sailed and joined the convoy. Several days out of New Jersey, as I was coming off the midnight watch, a terrific explosion shattered the silence. Night became day as an aviation spirit tanker two columns away was torpedoed and set the sea alight for at least a quarter of a mile around the ship. Oncoming vessels in the same column had to swerve sharply to avoid passing through a wall of flame. I heard that there were no survivors, and vessels passing close by could hear the screams of burning men, who had a choice of remaining aboard and being roasted or jumping into a blazing sea. That could haunt you for the rest of your life.

On my next outward-bound voyage I noticed an increase in escort vessels, and we also had an aircraft carrier. It was now the fourth year of the war, and the Navy was taking control of the seas, causing the U-boats to suffer unacceptable losses.

One of the tactics the Germans used was to employ long-range Fokker-Wolfe aircraft to shadow the convoy out of gunnery range and to transmit reference points back to the U-boat wolf pack. To combat this, some ships carried catapults for Hurricanes, which could be fired from the ship when enemy aircraft were sighted. It was the luck of the draw whether the aircraft had sufficient fuel to make landfall after completing its mission: the only alternative was to ditch in the sea.

A tanker explodes after being torpedoed. The aviation spirit tanker I witnessed engulfed the entire ship and part of the sea in flames.

Courtesy of the Imperial War Museum

Aircraft were always dispatched from carriers in daylight. Near the Newfoundland Banks I watched a Swordfish aircraft take off and circle. Five minutes later he came racing back, but by this time the carrier and convoy were enveloped in thick fog. We could hear the aircraft flying around the convoy all day long. Darkness was falling, and the aircraft must have been getting low on fuel when the pilot made a final attempt to land, and we heard a deep crash from the direction of the carrier, followed by silence. We all hoped that the pilots survived.

Enemy attacks on outward-bound ships were becoming more infrequent, and we made port safely. Before loading we steamed to Newport News, Virginia, in the Southern States, for annual dry-dock. I noticed a marked difference in behaviour towards the coloured population compared to the Northern States. Everything here was segregated, but I expect time has ironed out these differences.

Going ashore in the USA was quite a contrast to England. The country was untouched by the ravages of war, with no rationing or blackout. Some of the crew got evening jobs as dishwashers or packers and made more money than a week's pay. I liked the Americans: they were always helpful and generous.

The dry-dock repairs were finished in a couple of weeks and we loaded our cargo of 'lube' oil, as well as Mustang fighter planes and spare depth charges, which were secured on deck. We sailed and joined the convoy for the UK.

Five days out of port the convoy was attacked by U-boats wolf packs. They were finding it very hard to manoeuvre into firing positions because the increased

A Swordfish aircraft
Courtesy of the Imperial War Museum

A last glimpse as a torpedoed ship sinks stern first
Courtesy of the Imperial War Museum

escort formed more layers of protection and covered the entire area with Asdic surveillance.

Sound in the water is amplified. I was sent down to the chain locker below the water-line to get a shackle to secure a loose deck fastening for one of the Mustangs. While searching for this I heard the high-pitched whining of a torpedo, then a 'chink', followed by a sound as if a demolition ball had swung against the ship's side and hit the plate where I was standing. This was quickly followed by two more. Before I reached the deck again, with some haste, a ship in the outer column had disappeared. I was told that it was loaded with heavy ore. If a ship sinks so quickly there is little chance of survivors, as the suction from the vortex pulls everyone down. Even the freed oil drum life rafts strapped to the ship's rigging would be pulled under and would shoot to the surface minutes afterwards. I didn't hear of any survivors.

Some very odd tales were related to me by shipmates, previous survivors of torpedoed ships. In one unforgettable instance the crew had rowed to a safe distance and watched the ship disappear beneath the waves, when probably by some quirk of buoyancy or underwater boiler explosion, the ship's funnel re-emerged from the waves. The ship's whistle blew a final blast as the ship finally sank, as if saying a last farewell from a living soul.

All that night I heard the distant thud of depth charges. This continued on and off for several days. Then one morning all deck hands were called out to prepare the transfer of depth charges to a destroyer that was coming alongside. This was a hair-raising manoeuvre. A distance of about 30 feet had to be strictly maintained between vessels at steaming speed, which required the utmost concentration by the helmsmen. The depth charges were

A Hawker Sea Hurricane on the catapult of a merchant ship

A depth charge explodes astern of HMS Starling. Submarines tried to avoid the blast by turning sharply to port or starboard at the point of drop. The hedgehog cluster of depth bombs could be fired well in advance of the drop point.

slung across from one vessel to another by a derrick on each vessel and a connected sling. As we were working on this operation, an unexpected sea caused our side to slacken suddenly and slammed the depth charge against the destroyer's side, making quite a noise. At this point the destroyer's captain leaned over the bridge and shouted through the loud-hailer, 'That'll liven them up – got two of the swines last night and the crews are prisoners in there.'

One couldn't help feeling a tinge of sympathy for the nightmare the U-boat crews were forced to endure.

We completed the operation, cast off the sling, and the destroyer steamed back to station, charged for any further engagement with the enemy.

A salvo of 24 anti-submarine hedgehog bombs

Courtesy of the Imperial War Museum

Chapter 2

The Later War Years

At the end of the trip we docked in the London reaches, miles from any town. It was November 1944 and the Allied forces were well advanced. As I walked ashore and down a country road, some Chinamen from another ship approached from the opposite direction laden with parcels. Suddenly two Customs vehicles came racing down the road and the Chinamen took to the fields with the Customs men in hot pursuit. Chinamen always had a wary eye for business. I learned later that the parcels contained much-needed bicycle tyres for their cycling continent.

We discharged our cargo, I signed up for another trip and joined a convoy bound for New York. The war in Europe was now drawing to a close, and we experienced no enemy action on the outward crossing. We docked in New Jersey and loaded. After a couple of days there we found ourselves joining the homeward-bound convoy.

The laden returning convoys were now so well protected from the air that U-boats had little opportunity for a successful attack. Their only chance was to try and pick off stragglers who could not maintain speed and had to be left behind. The humming of the ship's engines became a natural part of the noise surroundings, and when this suddenly ceased we quickly became aware that something was wrong. The convoy steamed past until we

A Liberator aircraft, used in convoy surveillance duties

Courtesy of the Imperial War Museum

were left alone, and one of the escort vessels came along-side and enquired how long our engine repairs would take. Following the reply of 'several hours' we were in-formed through a loud-hailer: 'Sorry, I will have to leave you. Good luck.'

Very soon we were alone like a sitting duck without a ship in sight, and feeling like an absolute gift to the en-emy. The engineers worked frantically to repair the fault, and after a few anxious hours everyone was relieved to hear the thump as starter air entered the cylinders and the engine burst into life. Within a few hours we had caught up with the convoy, and I read a message from one of the escorts: 'Welcome back to the fold.'

I began to reflect on my fate. From 1941 I had come right through the war without a scratch. I wondered if I had used up my allocated span of luck, as some of my shipmates were in a watery grave, or ruined in health through spending many days in lifeboats. One of my shipmates spent forty-nine days adrift.

Safely back in Manchester, I joined the *West Point*, a tramp steamer with general cargo bound for Lisbon and the Mediterranean. Convoys were now seeing little enemy action, and we docked in Lisbon after a faultless voyage. This had been a neutral port all through the war, and a representative from the British Consulate boarded the ship to explain some of the strange laws under which one could at that time be arrested. One such was the use of a cigarette lighter without a licence!

If an enemy ship or U-boat docked at the same time as the opposition, the crews from the two vessels would not be allowed ashore together at the same time. Each took separate turns and would slang each other off as

A sad casualty of war: SS City of Benares, torpedoed in September 1940 while carrying ninety child evacuees to North America. Seventy-seven of them were drowned.

Courtesy of the Imperial War Museum

they walked ashore along the quay. Fortunately this did not happen to us.

The Portuguese were fiercely religious, but poor. Most would earn a pittance working in the fish factory and were proud to associate Britain with their history as their oldest ally. There have been no wars in the country, and all its antiquities were preserved.

We left Lisbon for Algiers and docked after several days with no incidents on the passage. After spending a week there, and as I was already familiar with the place, I thought it would be interesting to accompany some of the crew to one of the notorious French brothels. We were ushered into a plush reception room and the girls paraded before us as in a beauty contest. Some of the girls were of different nationalities, offering variety to the menu. Most of them had a story to tell: one was saving a dowry to be married, with the approval of her future husband. I asked her whether he minded and her reply was 'I can sell my body without selling my heart.' Some had been abandoned and had no other alternative to avoid starvation.

The worst cases were the innocent young girls who had been sold by their poverty-stricken parents in order to sustain the family. Social assistance was non-existent. I watched well-dressed men walk straight to the entrance of a stairway, pay their fees to the madam who was sitting at the foot of the stairs like a big fat spider, collecting the fares for sex. I had no wish to patronize any of these unfortunate girls, but left them a tip for an interesting evening.

The next day being Sunday, I took a walk into the town. The French are open-minded and it was not uncommon to see either sex using a quiet street corner

A British destroyer rescues survivors from a lifeboat of
SS City of Benares

Courtesy of the Imperial War Museum

as a public convenience. Neither was it unusual to see an Arab riding a small donkey with his feet trailing on the ground, holding a cane in case the speed slackened, while his wife lagged behind struggling with a huge bundle on her head.

By far the most amusing scene I came across was the sight of Arab farmers driving a small herd of cows with the bull running free with the herd. On coming to the crossroads to await a crossing, they were confronted by an immaculate traffic policeman in white uniform standing on a small platform in a prestigious position and directing the traffic. The policeman was using hand signals and a whistle and turning with all the grace of a bullfighter. He made a smart right turn, blew his whistle and beckoned the herdsman to cross. Half-way across the bull decided that one of the cows needed servicing, and in the process of performing his natural duty he stopped the whole line of traffic, causing huge laughter, horn-blowing and cat-calling of French love phrases at the policeman, whose dignity was ebbing as his face turned crimson. I have never seen its equal for amusement since.

The next day we left for Casablanca, loaded phosphate and joined the convoy for Liverpool. We experienced no enemy action and I left the ship there to take some leave.

The war in Europe was now over, but the 'pool' was still maintained, so I reported back to Salford and joined a tanker named *Voco* to sail to the USA and load lube oils. There was no need for a convoy, as the only danger was the odd floating mine near the UK coastline. We carried small arms, and when we sighted a mine on the outward passage, took pot shots at it as we passed.

We achieved our destination and loaded for Copenhagen. When we reached the Western Approaches our route took us through the Dover Straits at night, and lookouts had to be doubly vigilant because of the danger from floating mines. Although the North Sea minefields were cleared, there were still many reports of odd ones floating loose. Flashing green wreck marker buoys were everywhere. This was the price shipping had paid for navigating the Dover Straits during the war. There was the additional natural danger of the sand banks.

We proceeded up the North Sea with caution. It was a relief when dawn broke. That day we spotted a mine and took several rifle shots at it without managing to hit the horns and make it explode. After running this gauntlet it was a relief to see Copenhagen, where we berthed beside the German Navy, whose crews were playing football on the quayside. We viewed each other suspiciously, but strangely felt not a scrap of animosity between us. We could see that they were deprived of the usual requirements of social order – they were ill-fed, and were willing to barter anything for a cigarette, which was literally worth its weight in gold. When one of the crew who was walking ashore threw away a partly-smoked one, there was a mad scramble for the discarded dog-end.

Going ashore, we were immediately struck by the cleanliness of the city, which had experienced very little war damage. Surprisingly, bacon and eggs were available in restaurants, with the price being half a packet of cigarettes. I also saw motor vehicles running on pine logs. In spite of the war, the Danes had managed their affairs well and I found them to be most helpful. After Copenhagen we called at the port of Rouen to discharge the remaining part of our cargo before docking in Southampton.

At the end of this trip the crew and I signed off, I took some short leave, then made an uneventful trip from Cardiff to the States and back with coal in the *Empire Flame*. The important thing for me at the time was to qualify for 'sea time' to sit the examinations.

The elections produced quite a surprise when Winston Churchill was voted out of office and the Socialist Clement Atlee became the new Prime Minister. Many of the intellectuals from Oxbridge were sympathetic to the Soviet system, and when Labour politicians visited the Soviet Union and emphasized how the citizens owned everything, public opinion swung towards this Utopian theory.

It was at this point that I became interested in politics, and after reading some of the theory of Marx and Engels I must admit that I was impressed. However, I did feel that there was something missing: the theory completely extinguished individual freedom of expression, and the old adage of 'absolute power corrupts absolutely' crept into the equation. France and Italy came within a hair's breadth of becoming Communist countries.

With the new government in power in England the emphasis was on nationalization and export. I joined the *Fort Covington*, carrying general cargo consisting mainly of bales of cloth, optics and other valuable items bound for the Middle East. The entrances to all the holds on the ship were padlocked. On the passage down to the Mediterranean the crew quarters were at the aft end of the vessel below the old gun emplacement, and it was not long before a secret entrance to Number 5 hold via the old magazine was discovered.

While the mate was making his daily visual inspection of the padlocked holds, the crews were pilfering all they could carry into hideaway places, ready for businessmen in the ports the ship would visit. Some of the crew regarded this as one of the perks of the job. I wanted no part in thieving – which if discovered would blacken one's career prospects.

The first port we visited was Port Said, at the entrance to the Suez Canal. There was a delay in entering while we waited for a pilot to arrive. The seamen always called the first boat alongside the 'bumboat', because it was packed with items and souvenirs for sale. Its proprietors, who named themselves after popular actors of the day such as George Robey and Jock McGregor, would enter into an agreement with the Captain, in which a signed list of items purchased was given to the Captain. The Captain then paid the proprietor and deducted the necessary amount from the men's wages accordingly. One saw well-dressed Arab businessmen mixing with the bumboat crowd and carrying off parcels.

The pilot boarded and we started our passage through the Canal at the regulated speed to avoid our wash causing damage to the bank. When we reached the natural Bitter Lakes, halfway to Suez, our speed could be increased. Any loose ropes hanging over the side were an invitation for a free ride to small boats. Care had to be taken regarding thieves. I have seen poles with hooks coming through the portholes to hook hanging washing off the line – or anything else. Even the flies seemed to know in advance the instant of swat and would fly back on the same place. The whole spirit of the place seemed to revolve around making a living, from childhood to manhood, by any means possible. The numerous shoe-shine boys spoke three languages: I was quite surprised when passing the Army Officers Club to hear in Oxford English 'I say old boy, would you care for a shine?', coming from a small Arab boy. Once ashore you could not escape a shoe-shine.

There were no state handouts. I wondered why Egypt, with such a fine, ancient culture and history, was not more advanced in the present day.

We arrived in Suez, proceeded down the Red Sea and along the Arabian coast into the Persian Gulf, then north to the Shat el Arab channel that divides Iran from Iraq. We docked in Abadan in Iran to discharge mixed cargo. I was sure that some of the same Arab businessmen I saw in Port Said had followed the ship here overland. We discharged some cargo in low-draft barges, whose destinations took them into the many side waterways, where it was said that a fraction of the cargo disappeared without trace.

Our next port of call on the other side of the river was in Iraq. I found the Iraqis friendlier and many of the Arab boys spoke good English. However, when it was time to leave I was quite glad to quit the place to get into a cooler climate. We back-tracked through the Suez Canal and into the Mediterranean, to Italy and Venice, to discharge the remaining cargo. Venice I found to be a city of art works and felt indebted to the Italians for producing such talent.

We left Venice after several days, and when we finally docked in Glasgow I had achieved the required sea time to sit the examination for a foreign-going deck officer. By this time I was well into my studies, but wanted to enrol in King Edward VII Nautical College to work on the finer points. After attending the college for two and a half months, and becoming aware of the pitfalls in

The author as Third Mate, MV Baltic, aged 21

various questions, I felt confident enough to present my papers to the Board of Trade for the next examination. This was a week hence and a fee was payable.

The exam lasted for a week and comprised both written and oral tests, as well as examination of signals. The examiner stood on the platform and as the loud ticking of the railway station-sized clock was approaching the hour, announced that we could 'start on the precise minute' and that we should 'read the questions carefully'. He would stop us writing at the end of the allocated time, which meant that each question could take approximately half an hour.

I had never felt nervous at any time during the war, but this situation unnerved me considerably, although after a time I settled in. Not all questions carried equal marks: some carried several times the marks of others and these were usually the ones with pitfalls. The pass mark was 70%, so if you were tripped up by one of the pitfalls that carried high marks, you would probably fail the written exam.

Several days later I called at the Board of Trade to get my results. I was overjoyed to learn that I had been successful, and was given my first certificate of competency as a foreign-going deck officer. I decided to specialise in oil cargoes, and was offered a job with the Anglo-American Oil Company, given a rail warrant to Liverpool and instructed that the next day I would join the *MV Baltic*, a tanker of some 9,000 tons, as Third Mate.

Chapter 3

Shuttling Oil Cargos

When I arrived, the vessel was lying in Birkenhead docks while engine repairs were completed. She was an ex-German vessel with twin Krupp engines, and all her blueprints and notices were written in German. The Deck Officer's duty included loading and discharging cargo, so I had to familiarise myself with the pipeline and pumping arrangements – almost every tanker is different.

After engine trials were completed, we were ordered to proceed to the West Indies in ballast, to the refinery island of Aruba, to load fuel oil for New York. We left Birkenhead, dropped the pilot in Liverpool Bay and set course for Tuskar Light, Southern Ireland and thence to the West Indies.

Two days into the Atlantic we encountered severe gales and one engine broke down. The vessel was making much leeway in a southerly direction – something of which our very experienced Captain approved, as this was taking us closer to the Portuguese islands of the Azores, where there would be the option of engineering assistance if the ship's own engineers were unable to cope with the present problem.

As I came on watch the next morning, the first things I saw were the volcanic mountains of the Azores protruding straight out of the sea, with us heading for port in the island of Fayal. We moored the ship and the shore gang arrived to start work on the broken engine. Repairs lasted a week, during which I took time to go ashore. The people of the Azores were poor and strictly religious, to the point of preventing any fraternization with the local girls.

There was a dance and all the female partners were closely chaperoned on one side of the floor with the men on the other. In this tightly-knit community, which offered a livelihood of fishing, farming and a little whaling, with little scope for any ambition, the sexes were introduced to each other, usually through the families, in a long drawn-out courtship before marriage. Nonetheless, they appeared happy and warm-hearted and, being partly isolated, free from social contamination from the outside world. It would not be a place where I would choose to live – I would be concerned that the volcanic islands rising straight from deep water might some day revert back to the ocean depths.

The week passed quickly and it was soon time for an engine trial while moored to the quay. My docking position was the bridge telegraph engine controls, where I rang for full-speed engine at the Captain's order. The ship shuddered and a small explosion and huge ball of fire rolled out from the funnel as the engine climbed to full revolutions. After running for a couple of hours alongside the quay, we were told to resume our passage, so we cast off and set course for Sombrero Lighthouse in the Mona Passage through the West Indies.

A couple of weeks at sea gave me ample opportunity to practice the finer practical points of astral navigation. There was a degree of romantic satisfaction in this, especially when I was unable to take observations for a couple of days due to cloudy or bad weather. When nearing a landfall, just one snapshot of the stars could relieve much anxiety, and often produced a surprise. A ship's latitudinal position was ascertained whenever possible at midday, when the sun was on the meridian. This was the only way that mariners of the past were able to navigate, particularly the Spanish treasure ships of the New World. They would sail gradually north or south until they observed the same latitude as their destination, then travel east or west until they reached it.

This method was used until the marine chronometer arrived in the early nineteenth century and gave an accurate means of determining longitude. As long as the heavens remain in their prescribed cycle of motion, the principle of astral navigation is infallible. The Pole Star is also a remarkable body in the heavens and is located almost directly above the Earth's North Pole. It always points true north to within approximately one degree, and the angle from the star to the horizon is the approximate northern latitude. For example, if you saw the star on the horizon, you would be situated near the Equator.

Man has almost rendered astral navigation obsolete with artificial satellites and GPS. One wonders what would happen if the planet passed through a prolonged intense belt of meteorites that knocked out the satellites. Perhaps we would be right back at square one.

From our latest noon observation we calculated that we should reach our first landfall that evening, during my watch. At 9 o'clock I was delighted to report to the Captain that we were within sight of the Sombrero light. The light was well named, as it was shaped like a hat sticking out of the sea. We steamed through the passage with islands either side, where only a couple of centuries ago pirates were lying in wait, for vessels had to pass along this route to catch the prevailing westerly winds to Europe and Spain. Some of the treasure plundered and hidden must still be there. This area is also a frequent location for seasonal hurricanes, which probably claimed some pirate vessels too after their treasure was hidden, leaving none to divulge their secrets.

The lights of the refinery on the isle of Aruba were well visible from miles away at sea. On arriving there we docked, discharged the remainder of our sea ballast and began to load fuel oil. Within twelve hours the ship was fully loaded with 12,000 tons, and the docking pilot boarded and took us outside the harbour, wished us 'bon voyage' and disembarked.

We set course north for New York via the Mona Passage. As we passed through the passage close to the isle of Haiti, fires were visible on the hillside and distant chanting was audible, sounding similar to voodoo ceremonies, which were widely practised in the islands.

We spent a couple of days in New York discharging the cargo, and after that, several months trading between Aruba and the American coast. On several occasions our passage took us through the Bermuda Triangle, the notorious area noted for the disappearance of ships and aircraft. A magnetic anomaly exists in this area, as I experienced one calm evening, when suddenly the magnetic compasses started to spin in circles, and after a period, suddenly stopped. This is one of those occasions when observations of the Pole Star are useful for an instant check on compass error. The experience certainly spooked me.

We then received orders to proceed to Aruba to load fuel oil for Southampton – welcome news. After being away from home for long periods everyone is a little over-enthusiastic on the home voyage. The seaman's name for this is 'getting the channels', a feeling that becomes stronger as one gets nearer to port.

When we docked in Southampton, the Captain went on leave, but all the officers, including myself, signed on for another trip. A new Captain took over command of the ship, and after a week discharging our cargo, we received orders for Abadan to load crude oil.

This particular trip was to prove a cruise for the deck department and a nightmare for the engine staff. We left Southampton and as we reached the Bay of Biscay one engine broke down. While the engineers were working round the clock to repair it, the other engine failed. At the same time one of the main auxiliary generators that supplied the electrical system also seized up, leaving the ship helpless some thirty miles northwest of the Spanish coast.

The futile efforts at repair work continued for several days. Eventually the Captain radioed for tugs, which duly arrived and towed us into the Spanish Naval base at El Ferrol. At that time Spain was under the strict military discipline of General Franco, although we were allowed complete freedom to come and go as we wished. It was June, the season when fiestas were beginning in the small surrounding villages, so while the engineers spent several weeks working themselves into a state of complete exhaustion, the deck department was leading the life of Riley.

I was fortunate to find a Spanish friend who was fluent in English and who helped me with Spanish, and together we toured every fiesta. It was like being transported back to the English Middle Ages with the maypole, fair, firework displays, dancing and bands playing. It was good clean fun with plenty of alcoholic beverages, all costing next to nothing. I found the Spanish country people faultless and always willing to give us their last peseta.

The oil company, in the meantime, must have been getting concerned, as they dispatched an engine expert to expedite matters. After another two weeks we left El Ferrol and made for Gibraltar and through the Mediterranean to Port Said.

Just before we reached Port Said there was another serious engine failure, and we were towed into a mooring buoy dock adjacent to the Canal. We stayed there for two months with the engineers working flat out. Some of them were flown home on sick leave and replaced by others, while the deck officers were experiencing something of a Grand Tour.

It was emphasised by the Canal authorities that no repair facilities were available for vessels in transit and that they would allow no blockage of the Canal, so we had to ensure that our engines were in good working order before entering it. The oil company was concerned and sent out a German engine expert: after another week's repairs, they performed several hours of engine trials while the ship was tied to the buoys. Following this the Canal pilot was notified that we were ready to leave.

The German engine expert was sailing with us as far as Suez. We had interesting conversations together. He had left Germany during the Nazi regime and returned after the War to find his home town included in the Eastern Bloc. The very people he knew within the hierarchy of the Nazis now had similar positions within the Communist regime, so he left Germany and secured a job as international engine consultant within the company.

He also proved useful when we were passing through the Bitter Lakes, when I spotted two men clinging to a raft shouting for help. We stopped and picked them up. They turned out to be German ex-prisoners of war who spoke very little English, and following interpretation by our German engineer, we discovered that they were trying to make passage to civilisation. So they were fed and given the Good Samaritan treatment by their fellow countryman.

We arrived in Suez just before the next engine problems began. These were to keep us in Suez for another couple of weeks. It was some time before the vessel was dry-docked, and when we left Suez I noticed the growth beneath the water line was reaching a foot thick and rapidly increasing in tropical waters, reducing our speed to eight knots.

In this condition we proceeded down the Red Sea into the Arabian Sea, and thence through the Persian Gulf to Abadan, with alternate engines stopped for repairs. We loaded a full cargo of crude oil and returned in the same halting fashion to Suez, by which time the weed growth had increased substantially and reduced our speed to seven knots.

The crew were making bets with each other as to whether we could make a straight passage through the Canal. Surprisingly, we did make a trouble-free passage to Port Said, and lost no time in entering the Mediterranean. Two days into the Mediterranean we struck a severe freak gale which stove in one of the bow plates, and we had to steam into Malta for welding repairs, which took two days. We left Malta for the

Straits of Gibraltar and then on to Southampton, finally approaching the oil berth at the end of a trip of nine months that normally would have taken a fraction of the time. Almost the entire quay was lined with bowler-hatted officials from the London office ready to pounce aboard and question the various decisions made by heads of departments that lead to the trip lasting so long. After discharging the cargo we sailed to Antwerp for dry-dock and to hand the vessel over to the Belgians. I saw the ship two years later with a German crew.

The oil company was expanding and acquired bigger and more efficient ships that ran almost to the schedule of a bus timetable. I spent the next seven years shuttling oil cargoes all over the world, spending ten months of the year at sea and two months ashore. I was now Mate, single and unattached. Being at sea for long periods offered plenty of time for thought. During calm seas, being alone on watch at night hundreds of miles from civilisation is like wandering in the desert, and one's mind reaches out and reflects on all sorts of subjects. In particular our own solar system – how the Earth's axis is tilted to a precise degree, so delicately balanced, that gives us the seasons that produce the grandeur of life; our satellite, the moon that governs the tides and all the sea life. What lies beyond in other galaxies and solar systems yet unknown to man? It is a complete marvel, which leaves one gaping in awe.

Anyone worth his salt must have asked himself the ultimate questions, 'Why are we here?' 'Where are we going?' The leading intellectual in my day was Albert Einstein who, on being asked whether there was anything unknown that he would like to know about, replied 'The meaning of life' – but one is more likely to get a satisfactory answer from religion.

In my travels around the world I have seen enough evidence to convince me of the existence of a spiritual world, good or evil, with a different time dimension where death is not the end. So what is the role of mankind in the grand design of things? Trying to find the answer in science is like trying to measure infinity with an endless tape measure.

This became more apparent to me recently when listening to a talk on astronomy delivered in Truro Cathedral by one of the foremost astronomers of the day. His concluding remarks were 'We thought we would have the answer to many unanswered questions in receiving our data back from space probes. All we succeeded in doing was fragmenting a difficult problem into even more difficult problems.' He then turned to the priest and said 'I bow to theology.'

One is more tempted to seek an answer through artists or religion – areas without measure such as love, beauty, talent, truth and the prick of conscience, but history has shown that many conflicts of the past have been in the name of religion – as is evident at the present time. This was emphasized to me when Gandhi was touring India and came across an area of slaughtered people of a different sect. Turning to the culprits, he said 'You did this terrible thing, my children, because they called God by a different name.'

It appears the basic laws of life are written in stone in the Ten Commandments. One can only summarise the whole universe as being present with an infinite loving spiritual super-intelligence that is known by the Red Indian tribes as 'the Great Spirit', by the Arabs as 'Allah', by the Buddhists as 'perfect serenity' and in the West as 'God'. This is our God, of whom it is written that no eye has seen him (even in their mind's eye) but of whom there is a spark in each one of us, and who offers a perfect peace not to be found in the Earthly world. I am guided by the Christian faith and am content to leave it at that, and stop trying to put a definite value on something that has defeated many great scientific minds, both past and present.

Mankind is given free choice, and has reached a crossroads in history to pursue a path of discovery (including space and other worlds), made possible in the near future by unlimited power and scientific investigation with the aid of computers – or a path that could eventually lead to our destruction through the use of power in wars against ourselves.

Any alien visitor from the Cosmos today would view man as a malignant organism on a presently healthy Planet Earth, who has been directly responsible for the extinction of many species. My era has seen constant wars being fought somewhere in the world, with the worst atrocities committed during the post-World War II period. The planet's lungs are being damaged by the systematic destruction of the forests in the East and West, which in some instances took a million years to evolve. Some trees that have taken 300 years to grow are destroyed in fifteen minutes with a chain-saw, and the underlying topsoil washed away, endangering species of flora and fauna yet unknown to man that might provide potential cures for diseases.

Damage has been done to the ozone layer, where holes are apparently appearing, the sea and air are polluted by chemicals, but the worst act has been making nuclear explosions in the Earth's land-mass and atmosphere – in one instance puncturing the Van Allen belt without knowing the future effects. The purpose of man's disgraceful acts can usually be traced to political power and money. One can only hope our past is but a part of our evolution towards an awakening of full respect as a custodian of the planet – or perish.

The time had come for me to reassess my own situation. I was thirty years old and had to decide whether to continue in my present job, with financial security but ten months of the year spent at sea, and little prospect of a future family life, or whether to break free. My father lived near the Cornish fishing village of Newlyn, and during my leave I had developed an interest in commercial fishing, so when the oil company (now called Esso) sent me a contract to sign, I respectfully declined, thanked them and told them that I had no complaints but that...

...I've gone fishing!

*The Bonny Mary (PZ57) after being rigged out with
thirty baskets and approximately nine miles of long lines.
This picture also shows Newlyn harbour as it was in the
Seventies, with the long-liner fleet in port.*

Courtesy of Richard Major

Chapter 4

Gone Fishing

Almost literally stepping from the deck of a ship onto a fishing boat, I jumped straight in at the deep end. I bought a fifty-foot boat, the *Bonny Mary*, which was being sold by the Inland Revenue. I met the previous skipper, one Jack Williams, an ex-Royal Navy Petty Officer, who told me that the boat had been impounded from the previous owners by the Revenue.

I soon discovered that commercial fishing was very different from the Merchant Navy. After tinkering with drift netting for pilchards for a year without making much advance, I decided to place the boat in the hands of the local shipwright to rig her out properly for long-lining with a new side engine. Long-liners fishing within a range of a hundred miles usually had a small auxilliary engine in case the main engine failed. In the late 1950s, radio transmission was a luxury.

I thought it better to start at the bottom, and secured a berth as crew on one of the local long-liners, going to sea in poor weather with one of the hardest crews in the port. My first job: 'Get below and cut up the bait', which consisted of squid that had been iced for the previous two weeks, and whose fumes stripped all the paint off the fish-room. This, coupled with the smell of the bilge and diesel fumes, and the comparative violent motion of the boat, couldn't fail to make any newcomer sick, and

Newlyn 2003. One of the few remaining lively fishing ports. Long-liner fleet gone and replaced by gill-netters and beam trawlers.

Courtesy of Richard Major

I was no exception. I used to spew my heart out for the first day, which rendered me totally incapable of working. You would not get the respect of any crew member unless you could do the job, so you had to stick at your work, ill or not.

After a year had passed the work on the *Bonny Mary* was completed, and she was considered one of the best and strongest boats in the port. I had rigged her out with thirty baskets of long lines, overcome my seasickness and could work equally with any crew. I had also familiarised myself with diesel and petrol engines. If either of these stopped at sea, an instant diagnosis and remedy was necessary: failure to do this could result in losing the gear, or the trip.

Crews were hired on a share basis, in which no basic wage was paid, but everyone received a share of the catch after expenses were deducted – hence the term 'share fishing'. In this way, until the gear was shot, nothing was earned.

Naturally, generations of fishermen, from father to son, were not going to give away information about local grounds after they had lost gear in order to learn shore marks. A genuine fisherman would not tell lies – many were staunch Methodists – and there was no fear of thieves. A boat's crew of at least six or seven men longlining had to fit together socially. Some crews observed religion to the letter, and would not swear or put to sea on a Sunday, and would hold services aboard the boat between working hours. It would be difficult to imagine anyone who liked to drink and swear being a member of such a crew, and such men would generally find themselves a berth elsewhere.

I considered it better to hire a skipper who was familiar with the offshore grounds, while I would service the machinery. Working offshore summer grounds seventy to ninety miles from port could take three shots of gear – approximately twenty miles of line – lasting the week, and during the first year we scraped by with a bare living.

When we landed I used to enjoy fish and chips from the local café, which was run by the proprietor and his daughter, whom I used to admire. Joan and I soon became great friends, and twelve months later we were married. In November 2004 we celebrated our 47th wedding anniversary.

I am now in my seventy-ninth year, and upon reflection I would repeat the same path. We had our good and our worrying times, but the Christian faith helped us to weather the storms of life. Having a boat is similar to keeping livestock: it has to be tended constantly, and the engine maintenance and seaworthiness were always in mind. Local fishermen were quite versatile and many could turn to other occupations such as building, long-distance lorry driving or agriculture if prolonged bad weather or anything else deprived them of their fishing livelihood.

During the Sixties, boat's crews when hired were usually honour-bound to remain until Paul Feast (October). If they then wanted a change they could do so with goodwill. Nowadays everyone looks after their own interests, and if absent at sailing time, it is usually for a good reason.

I gained much of my fishing knowledge in this period, but you still learn after spending a lifetime in the job. Meticulous records from one year will be totally different by the next. Weather, tides and the movement of the Gulf Stream play an important part in sea fishing life. If the fishing gear happened to fall near a wreck there was usually an abundance of fish. Decca navigators, based on radio triangulation, were becoming affordable to hire, and the available books gave positions of World War II casualties and other shipwrecks.

As I glanced at Lloyd's World War II casualties, my eyes were transfixed by a name that seemed to jump out of the pages at me: '*Lagosian*, Latitude 25–35N Longitude 15–43W, Takoradi West Africa. Torpedoed, 7 crew lost' – my old boat. I wondered if any of the lost crew were my old shipmates. Even if given Decca readings of wrecks, it usually took many hours of grid searching to find the wreck itself. It was not always successful, either, as a Decca sometimes became erratic.

At that time it was skate and ray that formed the bulk of a viable lining trip: wreck fish like ling, conger and pollack made only a fraction of the money. So it was more likely in the summer that the skate and ray grounds were fished, but in the winter all fish made good money.

Jack Williams, who was a widower, asked me for a berth as one of the crew. He liked his glass of beer, was always in a financial state of 'stony broke', and could make suggestive remarks to the local belles, which were all passed off in good fun. The vehicle he drove was held together with bits of rope and Jack always carried a tin of half-smoked dog ends. He had a one-line nautical philosophy for every situation that arose. In all, a colourful character whom you couldn't help but like. I duly obliged him and he was with me in the *Bonny Mary*, which was named after Jack's late Scottish wife, for some time, until painful cancer took his life.

During one period when we were short of a crew member, I asked Jack's son Mike to do a trip with us. He had a reputation as a hard worker who was not averse to fairground prize fighting. Mike proved a good shipmate. We worked well together and we had a natural gift of persuasion with the men. He did a season with me and eventually went into partnership and did well, particularly in the winter, when it was 'hit and run' before the weather stopped the fishing.

The year of 1969 marked a point in Newlyn history as the 'Year of the Strike'. This was a period when unions were empowered to cripple industry with strikes based on the grievances of their members – referred to on the Continent as the 'British disease'. One of the main market stewards, probably versed in Marxist theory, got the sympathy of the fish workers and the backing of the biggest union and then demanded union recognition. Naturally, this was not acceptable to the merchants or fishermen in a share-fishing port, so a strike was called. This paralysed the outlets of fresh fish to the main markets like Billingsgate, stopped supplies and anything else involving sea fishing, and left the fishermen without a livelihood.

One morning, as Mike and I viewed Newlyn Fish Market stacked with prime fish and no buyers, we decided to buy the lot, load it into the *Bonny Mary* and chance finding a market somewhere else, which we did with the help of the main merchant, Mr. W. Stevenson. So that night we loaded *Bonny Mary* and slipped out of Newlyn bound for Swansea. A day later saw us approaching Swansea harbour entrance, which was controlled by locks. Fortunately for us, a coaster was entering the locks and we tagged onto his stern. The gate shut, locking us into the lock as well, and when the other gate opened and the coaster steamed out, we steamed out too, straight alongside Swansea Fish Market.

Unknown to us, union sympathizers had got word to Swansea that we were carrying 'black' fish, and they planned to trap us in the lock until we had dumped our fish load into the sea. Instead the fish was later sold and we recovered the costs, made a small profit and made passage back to Newlyn. We were pleased with our work that ensured that a number of fishermen's hard days at sea had not been wasted, although I did ponder on the near-disaster averted by luck and caused by the power of the union.

On arriving back at Newlyn, pickets were everywhere, and the weeks that followed saw a few pitched street fights and threats of violence. Merchant's lorries were followed to picket and threaten the receivers of fish, and various ruses were used to ensure loads got to the right destination. The seriousness of the matter was in some ways comical, as when one of the empty heavy transport lorries, with its tyres reduced in pressure and two leaking bins of fish ice placed over the drains, emerged from the fish packing stores en route for the usual markets. It was immediately followed by the mobile pickets, and when they had been drawn far enough away, the real loaded lorry departed unmolested.

This cat and mouse game continued, with each party watching the other. Then our fuel was stopped, but the union had not reckoned on the resourcefulness of the late W. Stevenson, who championed the cause of fishermen and on many occasions used one of his boats to supply all in need. The situation was looking like an embarrassment to the union, so as soon as they saw

A casualty of the Fastnet yacht race being towed in by the lifeboat

an exit strategy, they withdrew, and things got back to normal.

Mike and I worked the *Bonny Mary* well for a few years. There was always a laugh and joke aboard which made the work lighter. We both had sons in their mid-teens now and we took them to sea to familiarize them with the system. In 1978 we sold the *Bonny Mary* and bought the *Girl Patricia*, a bigger vessel that had recently been built locally. We carried thirty baskets of long lines stretching approximately nine miles. The set routine was to muster on Sunday evening and put to sea with a ton of bait, and land in time for Saturday morning's market.

Some time later, on arriving at the fishing ground a hundred miles from Newlyn, after shooting the gear, we heard an emergency weather announcement interrupt the radio program. The broadcast was aimed at those taking part in the Fastnet Race. Southerly gales of Force 10 were forecast as imminent for the area. Mike looked at me and asked 'What do you think?'. I replied 'If we leave the gear we shall never see it again.' So we decided to start hauling in the gear, which to our great surprise was loaded with fish.

As we worked the round, I had just finished cleaning my basket when Mike's younger son, who was just ahead of me, had to go below because of illness. I had time to make a drink of tea in the galley before taking my turn at the wheel. The seas were now as high as cliffs. As I poured the tea the boat lurched heavily and the sea came above the portholes. Mike stepped down from the wheelhouse looking as white as a sheet, for as the sea cleared the decks, leaving one crew member hanging with his arms around the mast and another clinging to the bulwarks, it was at that precise spot his son had been working ten minutes previously. The sea had taken three baskets of lines weighing about six hundredweight clean over the side – a narrow escape for the boy.

We continued to pick our way cautiously along the gear, and heaved a sigh of relief when the last anchor was boarded.

Looking at the chart, the Fastnet route appeared to go through an area of shallower water. Judging from the seas we were experiencing in deep water, the seas in shallower regions must have been tremendous. We soon heard a distress alarm activate, but we were too far away to render any assistance.

When we arrived back in Newlyn the next day we were lucky to have only lost three baskets of long lines. The Fastnet Race became a major news item. Lifeboats and helicopters did some splendid rescue work: some of the yachting crews had to jump into the sea to be rescued.

After a couple of days, when the weather became workable, word spread that a number of crew-less yachts were floating in the sea. Listening on the intercom between various boats and coasters, we heard them reporting floating derelict boats in their locality. An abandoned boat was a valuable salvage prize, and some boats did quite well from it.

The national press latched on to the story with a headline 'Sea Bounty Hunters'. Listening to one conversation from a boat being directed we heard 'Have located the craft but found someone on board.' 'Oh, bad luck' came the reply. This reminded me of the 18th Century wrecking laws, where if any living soul was found aboard, full salvage was questionable. It was also a reminder of the degree of callousness one can get drawn into when certain conditions arise. No amount of money could pay for those who lost their lives in that event. To this day I regret that we were not close enough to help them.

On very rare occasions during our fishing activities we would stumble on a casualty, usually a yacht or small coaster. In the early Sixties when winter fishing, if the weather was suitable we would often shoot the gear out in the evening in a safe spot, leave it, steam in, get a good night's sleep and muster at daylight. On mustering one foggy morning and steaming along the western shore of Mounts Bay to retrieve our gear, our dhan – a small marker buoy – was surrounded by flotsam, including bales of resin, from a small Spanish coaster, the *Juan Ferrer*, which had hit the Bucks Rocks during the night and sunk with severe loss of life. The lifeboat was recovering bodies. Two of the survivors had swum ashore, climbed the cliffs and alerted a farmhouse and the authorities. I felt deeply sorry for the orphans and widows caused by this accident. Thereafter a powerful light was installed on the nearby headland, Tater-du.

On another occasion when rounding Land's End in a northwesterly gale we came across an abandoned small coaster, *Sarb*, heavily listed to such a degree that the mast was hitting the water with every steep sea roll. It was impossible to get near the ship's side without risk of severe damage or loss of our boat, so we ventured near her stern to assess the situation. We could hear the engine still ticking over; life rafts and boats were still intact. Her cargo of steel rolls had moved in bad weather, causing the list. If we could get a line aboard it would only have required a mile tow to get her out of the weather under the lee of the land, but it proved too risky and she

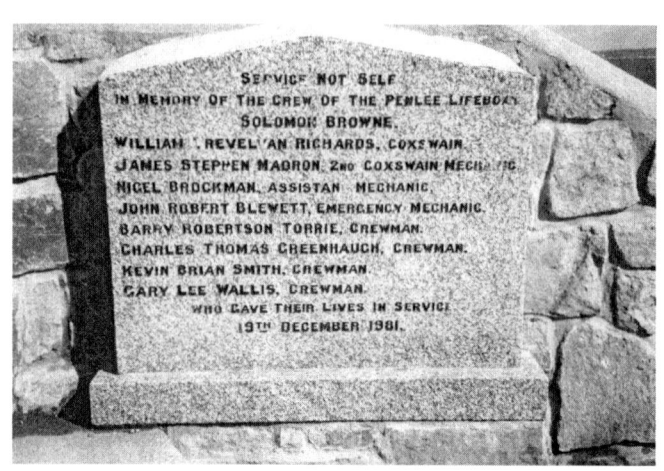

Plaque to the memory of the Penlee Lifeboat and her crew

eventually sank. Divers went down shortly afterwards and found little trace of her.

The worst casualty of all I partly witnessed from my bedroom window overlooking Mounts Bay. Being concerned for the safety of our boat moored in Newlyn harbour, at the high seas and run generated by south-easterly hurricane-force winds straight into the harbour, I observed distress flares. I phoned the coastguard, who had the situation well in hand. A vessel *Union Star* lay at the mercy of the sea to a lee shore with engine failure. The local lifeboat, *Solomon Browne*, and helicopter were called out to the rescue. The weather was so bad and winds so strong that the helicopter was unable to manoeuvre into a position of rescue; responsibility fell to the lifeboat, whose coxswain was well known to me as a previous shipmate in the *Bonny Mary*.

As I followed the proceedings, he was faced with an impossible task, of venturing close enough to the stricken vessel, now drifted into shallower waters with tremendous seas running, to rescue the crew. This was accomplished by the most extraordinary act of bravery and seamanship, and he managed to get clear with four survivors. Knowing of his determination, he returned to get the others left aboard.

When the radio went silent, the worst was feared and realized. The entire crew had paid the ultimate price in the attempt, and the episode is immortalized in lifeboat history as one of the finest acts of bravery.

The date, December 19th 1981, being so close to Christmas, the tragedy touched the hearts of the nation, and all sympathy was expressed to widows and relatives left to mourn their kin. I last saw the *Union Star* completely capsized on the rocks.

Shooting long lines from Mayflower. Three baiters and one shooter (the author).

After working the *Girl Patricia* for a couple of years we decided to get another boat. Mike would run *Girl Patricia* and I would run the other. We looked around for a suitable craft and found an attractive-looking hull advertised in 'Fishing News', so we travelled to the Mersey to have a look at it. It was strongly built in Norway, and we put down a deposit with the owner and arranged to tow her to Newlyn with the *Girl Patricia* when the weather was suitable.

Some days later we left Newlyn in the *Girl Patricia* bound for Liverpool Docks. We arrived at the lock gates a day later, entered the dock and moored. We wandered around this vast complex of one-time merchant ship cargo loading facilities, which had now deteriorated into a ghost of its past, with heaps of cargo slings piled everywhere – a casualty of technology and the introduction of containers.

We completed our business with the owner, who had been left the hull by his late father, and arranged to have her lifted in the water, leaving her for a day to swell the timbers before starting the tow back to Newlyn. Fortunately a Welsh fisherman generously offered to take us through the Menai Straits. We gladly accepted his offer, as this is a treacherous waterway with tides running at five knots or more, but it would save us a considerable distance. We passed through the Straits without incident, and two days later were glad to see Newlyn Pier with a half sunken hull in tow. We moored her safely and pumped her dry.

Mike worked the *Girl Patricia* while I rigged the gear and helped the shipwright with our other boat, which we named *Mayflower*. It took much longer than we expected to repair her and make her into a seaworthy long-liner,

Aboard the Mayflower

but eventually she was ready, and I worked her successfully from Newlyn.

One late winter afternoon Mike and I were proceeding to the conger grounds off Pendeen. I had chosen my spot, and the weather turned misty after we had shot our gear. As I lay to the dhan I switched the intercom over to Mike, who was ten miles to the north of us. To my surprise he had just recovered a floating life raft with fish boxes popping to the surface all around the boat. He informed the coastguard concerning his suspicion of a very recent unseen accident. The lifeboat was sent to investigate, and recovered a body, which by an extraordinary coincidence was identified as a well-known Belgian fisherman friend of a local fisherman and Penlee lifeboat coxswain. He had recently been here on holiday, and was on passage from Belgium on a northerly course.

A continental survey boat searched the area, found the wreck and sent divers down. They discovered the *Tornado*, which had been run down. There followed a lengthy enquiry to trace who was responsible for the accident. I did not hear of any more bodies being recovered, or the final outcome of the proceedings. I sympathized with the relatives, who were shocked to learn that their kin, seen just hours before, were now dead. But for the sighting of the life raft, their fate might never have been known.

Politics had now given access to Spanish lining vessels, which with less crew sharing could afford to have two crews working around the clock. They swept the grounds and long-lining became less viable in the South West. Most south-western long liners like us moved to the Holyhead dogfish ('dog') fishery. Mike's sons were

The wheelhouse of the Ben Loyal

now young men, as was my own son, so we decided to dissolve the partnership with a boat each.

After moving to Holyhead, I began to have misgivings about *Mayflower*, as things began to go uncannily wrong. Something always stopped me dead in my tracks, mechanically or otherwise, particularly when I had a good catch within my grasp. We moved back to Newlyn and put nets aboard. My son and I couldn't agree, so I withdrew and let him run the boat. Things began to worsen and caused me to think of the *Mayflower* as jinxed.

This may sound a little absurd, but during the war there had been such incidents, and one particular submarine with such a reputation was eventually lost with all hands. Every time the phone rang I had a sense of foreboding. I traced the history of the *Mayflower* and found that she had brought misfortune to previous owners, culminating in the last one who, after a disagreement with the harbour-master, had died in the wheelhouse.

The phone was ringing very early one morning. I knew it must be deep trouble to ring at such an hour, and was half-frightened to lift the receiver. When I did, the words 'She's gone' vibrated in my ear, then a sense of relief when followed by 'All the crew are safe.' I heard the full story when my son landed. The sea-cock had collapsed in bad weather, and with the vessel being very narrow in bilge, she quickly deepened in sea-water. Unable to stem the flow before the engine submerged, the crew had managed to transmit a distress call before the batteries lost all power.

The boat was insured, but not the gear we had lost. The bank would back us in getting another boat from the finest boat builders in the world, the Scots. We plumped for the 70-foot *Ben Loyal*, built by Hurd and McKenzie.

The boat has proved to be a very fine sea-going vessel which has proven itself in the harsh weather we experience here.

Chapter 5

The Decline of the Fisheries

During the late Nineties on passage, I had occasion to dock in Fleetwood. As I walked through the fish market, with grass now growing up through the auction floor, the eerie silence seemed to shout how our once-thriving hive of a fishing industry had been brought to the brink of extinction, and why so many fishing ports dotted around the British Isles, which were once part of community life, were becoming yacht marinas.

Reflecting on the past as a long-line fisherman, the main reasons were bad management and the rapid advance of fishing technology, but by far the major factors were politics and bureaucracy. During the last fifty years I have seen the demise of at least four different fisheries: the skate, crawfish, the Trevose season of mixed fish, and the mackerel and pilchard in our home port of Newlyn, one of the last bastions of commercial fishing.

One has to take an active part in commercial fishing to size the job correctly – this may take several years, learning secrets you are not going to divulge. A fishing boat skipper has more practical knowledge than a foreign-going merchant ship master. Each of these fisheries is a specialised job in itself, the gear's maintenance, plus an intimate knowledge of diesel engines, and the more recently added computers and hydraulics. The wheelhouse

*The catch of skate my son stumbled
upon when fishing for conger*

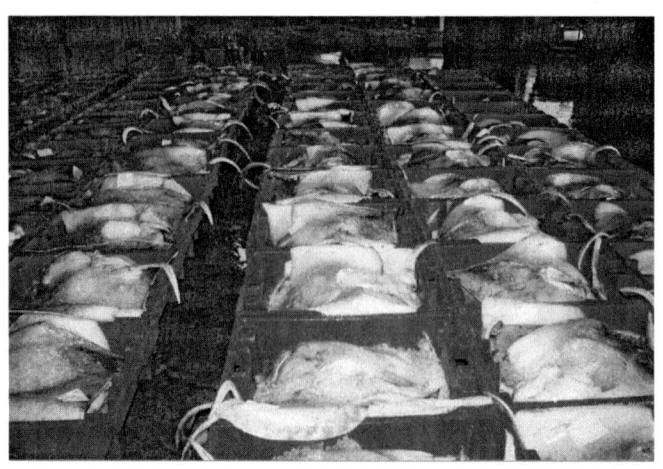

of the *Ben Loyal*, which our son, John, runs, is similar to sitting in a circle of computer banks.

The Skate Fishery

The skate fishery was a traditional Cornish long-line fishery, which I believe we are the last in the country to work when conditions are suitable.

This consists of shooting a total of eight to ten miles of long-line, stowed in baskets attached to strops off the main line, and each tied together. The hooks are bated as the lines are shot. The long-line is anchored to the sea-bed, with five to six thousand hooks spaced approximately eleven and a half feet apart, baited with mackerel, pilchard or squid, worked by two or three baiters and one shooter – which was usually me. Marker dhans are attached at various lengths.

It is the most conservational method of commercial fishing, since only grown specimen of hake, cod, ling, skate, ray, dogfish, sharks and so on are caught, leaving the marine environment undisturbed. It is also the only way of catching large quantities of conger eels. It takes two and a half hours to shoot and ten hours to retrieve, allowing a tide for feeding. This procedure is repeated several times to make a viable trip lasting a week.

This can be a dangerous job, as I have experienced to my cost. You have to pay out the line as fast as the tide is carrying you, allowing also for boat steerage-way. If you feel the line tighten beyond your control, as might happen if the boat is surfing in a following sea in bad weather, you cannot let go before taking a belaying turn – but failure to let go could easily result in being hooked or pulled overboard. If one is hooked and the barb exposed, it's an easy matter to snip the barb and remove the hook, otherwise it is razor-blade surgery. I think I have more line hook scars than anyone, as well as a missing joint of a finger.

Shifting ground in bad weather after hauling the gear, we would steam on to the Isles of Scilly to square away, ice and gut the fish in comfort alongside the town quay, where tourists would stare down in amazement as if we had just appeared from the Stone Age!

Within living memory the skate followed an annual pattern to enter an area off the Isles of Scilly in the springtime, where they would lay their eggs, then work their way into deeper water later in the year.

With the course of time, heavy continental stern trawlers began towing their trawls and disturbing the breeding grounds, and the skate started to disappear. Trawlers do not catch many skate, and I have not noticed many landed since the long-line fleet died out. However, some three years ago, my son, fishing for conger eel near deep water with a rough sea-bed, stumbled on an excellent catch of skate, much to everyone's surprise. Perhaps the fish had found an undisturbed rough patch to breed. It is consoling to know they still exists in numbers.

The only species nowadays that one can target with our traditional long-line method is conger eel, but the price has to be right before committing to the expense of catching them.

After the disappearance of skate, ling became a viable species. We would work the localities in rotation, which rested the fishing grounds. This continued for a couple of years, until one year on arriving we found Spanish monofilament long-liners working the grounds in columns for hake. They wiped out the ling as a by-catch.

When I complained to the Ministry of Agriculture, Fisheries and Food on the subject, I received a most polite reply stating that 'We must accommodate the Spanish in reciprocation.' In reciprocation to what, we never found out.

As we considered the remaining waters, Holyhead offered a hope as a dog fishery, as it had been left untouched for years due to its very strong tides. When they are feeding, dogfish go into a frenzy, so line hooks are placed as close together as possible, because one catches a fish on every hook. The gear cannot be baited and shot at the same time, due to the frequency of the hooks, but is pre-baited and packed ready to shoot at steaming speed into concentrations of dogfish, once located.

When we arrived at Holyhead in the early Eighties, the local newspaper was present with a photographer, pleased to get an unprecedented photograph of the Newlyn long-liner fleet in Holyhead. We learned to work the strong tides and the fishery became worthwhile. The locals were observing us making frequent landings, and that was a catalyst that seemed to set the place ablaze within the industry. Soon everyone was rigging dog lines, and for a few years a good living was made by some.

We were unable to work the highest spring tides, so we would return home, leaving the boat safely moored in Holyhead. During the mid Eighties boats in Newlyn were doing well with monofilament gill netting, so long-liners left Holyhead and switched over to gill netting. Gill netting has superseded long-lining, as it is less labour intensive, catches a more valuable species and reduces catching expenses.

East Coast steam drifters moored at North Pier, Newlyn in the early part of the 20th Century

Courtesy of Morrab Library

East Coast steam drifters moored in Penzance

Courtesy of Morrab Library

The Craw fishery

The shell fishery around the UK coast was the envy of the Continent. A small fleet of French crabbers was based here in Newlyn permanently. When pots were mainly used, crawfish were in far greater numbers than today, and the fishery was fairly sustainable over many years.

Then non-rotting synthetic fibres introduced themselves, in miles of craw nets, and almost instantly the crawfish catch multiplied. There was an outcry at that time from the shell fishermen, because skin divers were picking up the cocks in the shallower waters and thus depriving the berried hens of fertilisation.

Within three years the fishery as I knew it ceased to exist, and today just a few crawfish are landed. The lobster fishery suffered almost the same fate.

The Trevose Season

Every early spring, since time immemorial, fish of many different species, full of roe, made their way up the Bristol Channel to spawn, where a reception committee consisting of numerous Continental boats of all sizes awaited their arrival.

The boats from the local trawler fleet were docking during the Sixties full to capacity. The crews were exhausted in a comparatively short voyage, since at every haul the decks could not be cleared from the previous one, which meant working round the clock.

When working near these grounds one heard every European language being spoken on the intercom, and at night the whole area was alight like a town. The fishery of spawning fish was prosecuted so vigorously that each successive year the fishery declined, until today it is a fraction of its former self.

The Mackerel Fishery

During the 19th Century the mackerel fishery was well established and prosecuted by local boats and East Coast steam drifters. When the railway came to Penzance it provided access to a ready market to London, and the East Coast men had no qualms about being at sea on a Sunday to catch the market. This went directly against the religious principles of the locals and led to riots, and the Army was forced to intervene to quell them. This is how the saying 'Holy Mackerel' originated. I have a painting entitled 'Armistice Day in Newlyn, 1918' that depicts many East Coast mackerel drifters dressed with flags. I can only assume they were engaged in the now non-existent Plymouth herring fishery.

After Christmas the drifters would start to arrive and search from Wolf Rock out to the 200-mile limit to locate the shoals, which they did from signs gleaned from long experience, such as the colour of the water and the behaviour of birds, arriving back at Newlyn with a catch graded as 'fresh', one night iced or two nights iced. When the sample was placed on the auction table, the congregation of fish buyers, salesmen, began the bidding with winks and nods, much to the amusement of the spectators, some of whom were hoping for a free sample.

The drifters would work from Newlyn until May, or until the more attractive herring fishery opened in the North Sea. Over the years they took casualties, being caught in storms; when I started my fishing career in the late fifties, the talk of Newlyn was the loss of the drifter *Playmates* with all hands.

About this time the seasonal East Coast drifters began to arrive in lesser numbers for every consecutive year, until the time arrived when the last drifter left Newlyn with the customary farewell on the ship's horn, but this time it echoed the end of an era.

A remark made by a skipper, 'My crew have caught more mackerel on hand lines last trip than our fleet of nets' was the prelude to a new mackerel-catching industry, the hand line. This did not require expensive initial outlay, just fifteen to twenty angling-size hooks tied on to feathers or thin tubular plastic strips, spaced and tied evenly on to approximately twelve feet of strong gut, which was then weighted with two or three pounds of lead weight. This gave one a stake in the fishery at very little cost. The crew always left one line in the water, alternately cleaning the line of fish and casting. This was important to keep the fish in the locality when in a feeding frenzy, and also in not getting the line tangled, which could interrupt the process.

Fishermen are great innovators: soon things began to run more smoothly with the introduction of the 'girdy'. This consisted of a wheel on which the line was wound when hauling, preventing entanglement. When this graduated to the 'stripper', a system of pulleys that stripped fish from the line, the catch was increased considerably.

During the late Sixties and early Seventies, huge shoals of mackerel began to show on the echo sounders within a hundred miles of Newlyn. First onto the scene were the Russians, with their big processing and catching fleet. They were at pains to avoid any interference with our long-line marker dhans if working in the vicinity, as if they were unable to believe their good fortune at

The Rarau firmly wedged on the Seven Stones Reef.
She was shortly to share the fate of the Torrey Canyon.

Crown Copyright, Ministry of Defence

having access to the fishery, and had no desire to create incidents.

All went well, but not without mishaps: such was the enthusiasm of the catchers that if one tuned in to the right frequency it sounded as if one was listening to a recording of Polish fighter pilots during the Battle of Britain.

One morning, on returning to our fishing grounds, we saw the catcher *Rarau* sitting squarely on the Seven Stones reef. Whatever story circulated, it was all too evident to us what had probably happened – with his high-powered sonar, he had mistaken one of the Stones for a dense fish shoal. It must have been quite a surprise when the vessel ground to a halt. Fortunately there was no loss of life, and as the weather was fine for the next couple of days, a team of Russian technicians boarded the vessel and removed all electronic equipment. Then she was left to join the *Torrey Canyon* and other wrecks, which she did.

I felt sympathetic, and often wondered about the fate of that unfortunate skipper for committing the cardinal sin of destroying state property.

Their access was short-lived, as the 200-mile limit soon came under international law that excluded the Russians. It was a godsend when, from about the Sixties onwards, the mackerel shoals began to appear between September to March around the Falmouth side of the coast.

The hand-line fishery of late August reached its high-light in the Seventies. Our previous boat, the *Bonny Mary*, was one of the first to prosecute the fishery. During the winter months when the prevailing westerly gales prevented us from long-lining, one found a lee from

The Last Stop.
'Princess Anne', one of several displaced trawlers from
Icelandic fishing grounds, looking totally out of character
against the background of St. Michael's Mount, fishing in
Mounts Bay. On noticing a flock of gulls over her stern, one
skipper was heard remarking over the intercom
'Where do we go from here?

Courtesy of Richard Major

the weather under the shoreline of Falmouth and usually managed a fine day's fishing of top-quality mackerel.

Soon other boats began to arrive: in three or four years I saw two, three, four and five-man crewed hand-line boats stretching to the horizon in any direction. Our best catch for the day was eight tons. It became almost a nine-to-five job based at Falmouth. There were some odd modes of fish-carrying vehicle in the morning lines of traffic along the Penzance to Falmouth coast road, as fishermen liked to transport their own catch back to Newlyn whenever possible. I saw one enterprising fisherman driving a disused hearse on the return journey, fully laden with the boxed mackerel neatly stacked on the coffin board, conveying them to their last resting place in Newlyn Fish Market with an air of dignity usually associated with those who have passed on.

One could hear strange accents over the VHF – even those of professional people: teachers or technicians who were fed up with the rat race jumped onto the mackerel wagon. The local dole queue reduced considerably. The huge shoals remained static and were milked vigorously week after week without being diminished. Sometimes you wouldn't think there was a mackerel in the sea, with no marks or signs, then when the tide turned suddenly everyone was catching, and echo marks appeared everywhere. This happy situation continued for a few seasonal years.

There was a ready market for top-quality selective mackerel, and if you started to catch smaller fish you simply moved ground until you caught large ones. The sea-bed was kept clear of the few discards by crabs and other bottom-feeding fish.

The back of a lorry collapses, resulting in a road block of mackerel from an industrial trawler. Multiply this many times to get a picture of the sea bed from Start Point to St. Ives Bay.

Courtesy of Richard Major

Alas, this was not to last: potential wealth was there to plunder. Arriving on the grounds one morning we were surprised to see two huge trawlers – deprived of their Icelandic fishing grounds – towing for mackerel off Mounts Bay.

Scottish pursers and other freezer trawlers capable of taking a few hundred tons at a time soon joined them. These were later accompanied by huge Russian freezing, canning and processing ships that took much of the catch. Every year saw an increase in high-powered vessels equipped with the latest technology, including powerful sonar.

The slaughter of the mackerel reached alarming levels, so a quota was applied to each vessel. This measure exacerbated the problem and resulted in large numbers of smaller mackerel being dumped to achieve a quota of larger fish. Freezer trawlers that caught in excess of their freezer capacity simply dumped the surplus. Soon the sea-bed was littered with dead mackerel from Start Point to St. Ives Bay, creating pollution and depriving other fishermen of their livelihood. I pointed this out to the Ministry – whose response was a request for a sample in case the fish had died of some disease.

The Dutch had also tagged on to the scene early on, and were quietly decimating the outer shoals, receiving a prize and congratulations from the EEC for export. This praise was later retracted when it was discovered that they had over-exported their quota.

In the Eighties, when the season came round, boats converged from all corners of the UK to the 'promised land' of the South West mackerel. The fresh market was saturated, so the fish was either canned or sent for meal, and when boats could not be unloaded in time the local

Pilchard unmeshing in port, mid 20th Century

Courtesy of Morrab Library

farmers took the catch to use as fertiliser. Ministry officials were present to check on quotas, as purse-seine netters, 'pursers', were landing their catch onto Russian processing ships. Even when the mackerel fleet was observed in sight of Falmouth Cliffs, like some military task force in operation, it was impossible to monitor.

One evening in Mounts Bay I counted forty boats – pursers, catchers and freezers, all with high-powered sonars – searching for the broken shoals. These vessels were banned from fishing inside the three-mile limit. When threatened, fish species seem to have an innate instinct for survival, so I was amazed to see the mackerel lying within the three-mile limit, forming an almost perfect contour with the shoreline.

This did not save them: boats were still caught fishing inside the limit with their lights out. It became obvious to everyone that no fishery could sustain such an onslaught. Divers reported masses of dead fish on the sea-bed and guessed that much of it was dumped as waste.

On reflection, the obscenity of the mackerel fishery, and the needless slaughter of fish, can be compared with the recent Foot and Mouth fiasco in the farming industry, during which healthy animals were slaughtered needlessly. However, it did result in one of the finest pieces of conservation legislation ever to come into force, in the shape of the South West 'mackerel box' – an area of sea in which mackerel fishing is not allowed, with a derogation for the hand-line fishery – in which the scientists played a constructive part.

Over the years various unsuccessful ruses have been tried to penetrate the box for short-term profit – usually by newcomers who fail to appreciate the importance the box has to the marine food chain, and in keeping

Went out to wash nets in Mounts Bay and boarded another catch

Courtesy of Morrab Library

overspill to other sectors. Sadly this has now been compromised by a political decision to allow industrial fishing in the box for other pelagic species, so defeating its purpose.

Two of the casualties of this fishery in bad weather were the *Bounteous* and the *Boston Sea Ranger*, both with severe loss of life.

THE PILCHARDS

Drift-net fishing for pilchards is a centuries-old Cornish tradition. It was a thriving export industry in its early days, canning pressed pilchards in wooden casks for export to Italy, and for pilchard oil, which has health-giving properties. I am surprised that it was not commercialised on the same grounds as cod-liver oil, as the medical profession never tires of expressing the benefits of fish oil. The local shipwrights maintained that boat timbers impregnated with pilchard oil would never rot.

I did a season at pilchard catching just before the end of traditional drift-netting. This was caused mainly by the shoals moving out of range into deeper water, as well as by imports from the massive South African pilchard industry.

The industry has not entirely died out here at Newlyn. The two main canning firms have gone, but many of the pressing tanks are still intact. One firm still takes an active part in exporting excellent wooden casked fish and producing pilchard oil in the traditional way, supplied by two small ringed-net boats. It also provides a tourist attraction and museum where people can take a tour of the factory and view a trade carried out in the traditional way. There is now a program to promote the industry as the 'Cornish Sardines' that they really are.

Excellent produce from the present day factory at Newlyn

Chapter 6

Advances in Fishing

Commercial fishing has not escaped the technological age, and has in some ways contributed to the decline of the fish stocks.

In my own field we installed the Mustad system of long-lining, which has the advantage of automatic baiting, enabling the gear to be shot at far greater speeds. It does not require a man on the side deck unhooking, as the fish is stripped off the hooks automatically. A couple of East Coast vessels became very successful with this, but we failed, because our boat was not suited to its accommodation.

We did have a narrow escape when working this system. Hauling the gear was automatic, and the line was guided into a 'shoot' and stripped of fish, which fell into the fish hold. The man controlling the hauler could tell when he was coming to the end of a tier by the proximity of the marker dhan, which indicated that he should slow the hauler and listen for the bounce of the anchor against the boat's hull. At this point the hauler was stopped, and the anchor lifted inboard.

On one occasion, on one of the last few hooks was a hand-grenade, neatly hooked through the pin, which fell on the deck and was quickly thrown overboard. Our gear must have fallen near an ammunition dump. Had this been hooked further along the tier and had we followed

Our boat Ben Loyal, showing the hydraulic hauler

the procedure, the stripper would have pulled the pin and the grenade, armed, would have rolled into the fish room! This incident caused me to ponder the theory that one's life is already mapped.

This was a narrow escape, and we reverted back to our traditional way of shooting and baiting at the same time, and targeting conger eels only when viable. We had no complaints with the Mustad system, which did everything it claimed, but catching many fish of little value, it was hardly economic.

As gill netting is more profitable, there are no longer any boats in Newlyn doing full-time long-lining. Since manufactured monofilament gill nets increased the catching power for valuable species such as hake, turbot and monkfish, this is now the main method used in Newlyn and on beam trawlers.

Within the last fifty years, fishing electronics has taken a quantum leap. Asdic was developed by the Navy for use in anti-submarine warfare; sonar was a follow-on from this, consisting of a high-powered electronic impulse projected into the sea. Upon striking an object, echoes are sent back and displayed on a screen. Some now have a range of several miles. Incidentally, whenever high-powered sonar or exploratory seismic explosions are used in the sea, it affects the fishing considerably, and also sea mammals, which have evolved a highly sensitive receptive system – it must interfere with their natural homing by disorienting their brains.

During the late Fifties, boats that did not have one of the early Decca radio direction-finding sets to navigate relied on gadgets that are now collectors' items. Decca, although sometimes erratic, enabled boats to work wrecks and rough grounds, and was particularly valuable to trawlers in avoiding sea-bed obstacles.

Later Decca was superseded by GPS, the Global Positioning System. For fishing purposes this gives accuracies to six feet anywhere on the planet. When combined with the latest echo sounders, it gives almost a photograph of the sea-bed, which can be replayed at any time and enables return to the exact spot. There is therefore now hardly a metre of sea-bed that is unknown.

Dhan lights are now obsolete, as a searchlight on the reflector locates the dhan. This has many advantages – not having to worry about position in fog, for example – and working with radar has reduced much of the danger.

There is another side to this coin. By merely noting a few numbers, particularly the locations of wrecks, guarded local grounds were revealed that had been handed down through generations of fishermen by the location of shore marks. Rough grounds in which no trawler dare venture were penetrated, reducing the number of natural sanctuaries for fish, and of breeding grounds for some species in migration.

Communication has also advanced, and we can now even send faxes from the boat.

Hydraulics made a major improvement and was the key to working gill nets, both in retrieving and handling. Without our hydraulic hauler, it would not be possible for our nets to fish the depth of water or to work the length required to make a viable trip with the minimum crew. Hydraulics is also invaluable as an engine transmission.

There is a piece of waste ground in Newlyn where redundant fishing equipment is stored, and sometimes people come to look at objects from the past that have been replaced by hydraulics, discarded by fishing boats or brought up from the deep. Some of these items are now collectable, like old sailing ship anchors and aeroplane wreckage.

Gear made from natural fibres absorbs water, becomes heavier and naturally rots, so that it always needs conserving – barking, tarring and so on. When synthetic fibres appeared, it was little wonder that they were immediately adopted by the fishing industry. With stronger gear one could take extra risks without so much fear of losing it.

More powerful engines were also developed, and soon Dutch trawlers were using well above 1000hp. This meant bigger trawls, covering more ground. The bigger the boats, the bigger the expenses – fuel, ice, communications, food – and the greater the catch required to make a trip worthwhile. Even our own seventy-foot boat, on any five-day trip, clocks up £2,000 in expenses.

Fishing vessels are now built that are likened to cruise ships and which fish internationally. I cannot see grounds within the 200-mile Continental limit that can sustain economic operation for such vessels, except in very deep water, catching uncommon species.

The emphasis in fishing technology has been mostly on the catching side. Man has now reached an unprecedented point in fishing history, where his catching ability in the oceans has overtaken the ability of fish to replenish itself. So the most efficient way of catching fish is not always the best when it comes to sustaining a healthy stock.

Bad Management

We once had a Ministry called 'MAFF' – the Ministry of Agriculture, Fisheries and Food. In its early days it managed fisheries both at sea and inshore, and incorporated the marine scientific sector with survey vessels, as well as agriculture.

I was once invited to a meeting with MAFF civil servants that opened with the following remark by the speaker: 'I'm afraid I don't know anything about fishing, but I am an authority on farming, which is almost the same thing.' I was speechless at this remark. Commercial fishing is not identical to farming. You do not get a crop of fish every year, good or bad. It takes some species between five and thirty years to grow to their full size.

In this respect scientists play a significant role in ageing and tracing the migratory habits of fish stocks. The diurnal movements of the warm waters of the Gulf Stream also plays an important part in this. I have seen Gulf weed close to the Isles of Scilly, similar to that which you would find in the Florida Straits. I once even witnessed a marlin leap straight out of the water two miles from Wolf Rock.

The temperature of the water also coincides with the location of tuna, which has been moving gradually north over the past few years. The traditional way of catching these, used by Spanish fishermen, is with poles and lines steaming at speed. In the Pacific crews line up on either side of the boat with strong pole rods, casting the bare barb-less hooks and heaving in the tuna. The tuna fall off the hook themselves and the catching is non-stop. The most important man in the boat is the 'bait-man', who is responsible for keeping the bait, usually anchovies, alive in tanks.

When the tuna shoals are spotted, which may take days, the bait-man bails the bait into the shoal, keeping the fish in a feeding frenzy so that they will bite the bare hooks. Modern tuna boats, which are up to 200 feet or more, work internationally, are fitted with a helicopter pad, and use huge ring nets.

We worked the tuna fishery with tuna drift nets, which was encouraged by the government of the time to take pressure off other fisheries. The French had a much larger drift net tuna fishery than the men in the South West, so the Spanish, fearing for the continued existence of their traditional fisheries and aided by the Green Party and the by-catch of dolphins, successfully pressured the European Union for a ban on tuna drift nets from 2002. This meant that all the money spent on nets and rigging for the tuna fishery was wasted. Our EU partners were compensated, as we too were promised, but like most of the Government's promises we received nothing, instead being told that the South West was entitled to Objective One money.

A modern Spanish ring net tuna vessel has the capacity to catch more tuna in a single cast of its net than the entire Cornish drift net fleet in the whole season.

SUPPORTING THE HATCHERY

When scientists work with fishermen it can avoid some of their painstaking work being brought to nought. A case in point was the release of small lobsters off the Isles of Scilly – straight into the mouths of waiting predators, sea bass. Local fishermen know that these predators are inactive at night, so a release at night would have been far more productive. Such local information could be applied in the release of other species to achieve a mature survival rate. The United Kingdom has some of the finest shellfish grounds in the world which, if managed on the same basis as used by the Canadian Fisheries and Wildlife Authority, could produce great wealth.

Although scientists play an important part in fish stock management, they are not always right. I have never met any who could earn a livelihood at commercial fishing, and by doing so naturally glean information from the fishermen. In this sense fishing is as much an art as a science, and experienced veteran commercial fishermen with a lifetime's wealth of knowledge should be recruited in an advisory capacity, particularly with regard to methodology and the marine environment.

MAFF and the industry seemed to co-exist quite amicably up to the point when we joined the EEC and signed up to the Common Fisheries Policy (CFP) and the Common Agricultural Policy, when our law became subordinate to EEC law. Thereafter fishery policy was dictated by Brussels, and when Spain entered the EEC a new dimension was added to the scene.

One of the first acts of the Spanish was to re-register as set-up brass-plate British firms and so gain access to UK waters, quotas and grants. This was condemned at the time by our fisheries minister, legislation was introduced, and the Spanish were removed from the register. This left them nowhere to work and they took their case to the European court as the 'Factortame' case.

This finally ended in the House of Lords, which ruled that European law over-ruled Parliamentary law. So the years lost in fishing time gave the Spanish a huge compensation claim against the Government and returned their right to British registration, now known as 'flag ships'. I have watched them landing at Fleetwood straight into Spanish freezer lorries bound for Spain, giving little financial benefit for this country. Fish merchants have told me that Spain has switched from being an importer to an exporter of fish.

After Spain joined the EEC its large fishing fleet was looking for grounds to work, as negotiations of access to European waters were not permitted until the transitional period ended. During this period Europe provided a solution by buying fishing rights for Spain in Third World waters, partly financed by the British taxpayer. We have seen incidents portrayed on television between Spain's industrial boats and the local fishermen, particularly in Mauritania: locals are complaining of fish stocks being wiped out, and no doubt pressurising their governments to end the Spanish fishing rights. Should this happen, it poses the question 'Where do they go from there?'

Since Europe has controlled fishing policy in the CFP, an admitted disaster by its architects, an endless stream of useless paperwork seems to have appeared. Total Allowable Catch (TAC) quotas were introduced with logbooks, which had to be strictly complied with on pain of Draconian fines for the flimsiest of offences.

We became a victim ourselves when my son landed with Ministry officials present. He thought it unnecessary to inform them that he had arrived, then returned to sea to retrieve his gear before the forecast storm broke. This also occurred on two other occasions, when we arrived late or early – for many reasons, one cannot predict an exact time of arrival. I was called to an interview and thought that would be the end of such a trivial matter.

Almost twelve months later I was surprised to receive a summons to Court. The magistrates heard the case, and the prosecution stated that each offence carried a fine of £50,000. In my defence I pointed out that there was no attempt to conceal any fish and that Ministry

A beautiful Scottish-built boat

officials were present. Our only offence was being late or early, for which we pleaded guilty and hoped that their worships would see the reality of nothing.

They retired to consider their verdict for an hour. When they returned to pronounce the verdict I was hoping that the wisdom of Solomon might have influenced their judgement. No such luck. 'Mr. Turtle, each offence carries a penalty of £50,000. We are fining you £1,000 for each offence, a total of £3,000 plus costs.'

At this point the quotation 'Whom the Gods destroy they first make mad' came to my mind. I wondered whether our judicial system, now administering European law to the letter, apparently in the hands of bureaucrats ignorant of practical commercial fishing, is inadvertently dispensing justice of the kangaroo variety – or at least embarking on that route.

I realised that this could be a deliberate ploy to pressure the UK fleet into shedding more boats from the industry, so allowing room for other countries with fishing fleets about to join Europe. At present the area administrators are investigating proceedings, costing thousands of pounds, and involving merchants and fishermen, with a zeal that would be applicable to the Watergate scandal. They are seizing fish records from boats and the chain of sales to the retailer to prove that prime fish that was marketed should have been returned to the sea dead – all in the name of conservation!

If found guilty those involved would be subject to the heaviest of fines, which would be ruinous to fishermen and merchants. This is already being labelled 'Newlyngate'. Fishermen are being harassed to the extent that the local press are calling Newlyn a 'police state'. Not content with that, the National Audit Office has

The same boat later, after bureaucratic vandalism took control. Many fine boats, including Bonny Mary, suffered a similar fate.

revealed its ignorance of the practicalities of commercial fishing by approving this action and stating that the Government is not doing enough to detect and prosecute fishermen who land fish illegally.

It is certainly achieving the result of pressurising fishermen to leave the industry, and the recent sweeping ban on the cod fishery in the North Sea as a conservation ruse will provide an exodus, mainly from Scotland, of those who have been given the next round of decommissioning money. 'Decommissioning' is Government money provided on an auction basis of so much per unit or tonnage. A certain amount of money is provided for an area, and those boats that are least costly to decommission are successful, until all the money is used.

In our particular area, this means 'none'. To qualify for decommissioning, you must have your Sea Fishing Safety Certificate with full Category A licence to date. You surrender your licence to the Ministry, and the boat must not re-enter commercial fishing. This can be assured by destruction – or by using it as a memorial.

Since it is the licence alone that governs the fishing effort, it is quite unnecessary to destroy the boats. It has been heartbreaking to watch bulldozers on the slipway smashing good sound boats that took skilled shipwrights months to build, and which could easily have been converted into fine sea-going yachts or houseboats, augmenting the fisherman's income on his departure from the industry. Sheer ill-conceived bureaucratic vandalism to which there seems no redress is leaving no trace of our past in boat-building techniques.

Is this the fate of the British fishing fleet?

Laws written in EU treaties create problems. 'Relative stability' can be interpreted as meaning anything, but as far as fishing is concerned, it means that the catching power does not exceed the rate of fish replacement.

The EU has jurisdiction over the tonnage of the EU fleet and has ruled, usually on scientific and political advice, on a cut in tonnage across the board, with failure to comply resulting in a heavy fine for the offending member state. The UK has been the worst hit over the years, has implemented several decommissioning schemes to comply, and has reduced its fleet to the present level.

One of the first concerns of fishery management should be the sustainability of species, having due regard for the marine environment in which they live and breed. Many of the rules applied have been in the name of conservation, but there seems to be such a degree of ignorance amongst the conservation body that one has to conclude that the heavy weight of immediate short-term profit and political convenience dominates the central theme.

The authorities might stir into action when by-catch casualties like dead dolphins washed onto a beach provoke public opinion. Such an example is the current French high-powered pair trawling for bass with trawl capacities large enough to hold several jumbo jets. What kind of fishery can sustain this? It could also have a long-term effect on angler fishing.

Another example is industrial fishing in the North Sea by the Danes for animal feed, thereby making a positive contribution towards wiping out the bio feed for cod and other species. Some scientists have supported industrial fishing on this side of the Atlantic, usually where their employers have a vested interest, but on the other side the completely opposite opinion is held by responsible sea fish bodies.

Over the years, when various new fishing methods have been tried, proven profitable and implemented, no matter how damaging to the marine environment, it is unavoidable that each will eventually become unviable – because if you do not exploit it, others soon will.

There is a simple way to ensure sustainability: do not catch small fish. This is easier said than done. There has been some success with control of mesh size, and it is illegal to land undersize fish in the UK. Walk around La Corunna fish market, however, and you will find that the Spanish target small fish as a delicacy. When the BBC's Robin Cook travelled there to film just how the Spanish played on our 'level playing field' for the Cook Report, he was lucky to escape with his equipment.

There is no will amongst our European partners to enforce any fishing rules. I cannot imagine any of the Continental member countries, particularly the French and Spanish, being hounded, investigated and put through Court procedures such as those we have recently experienced. There are more Ministry officials in the South West of England alone than all those for the entire Spanish fleet.

Safety Regulations

Safety and life-saving appliances were first regulated by the Board of Trade, then the Department of Trade and Industry, and currently the CGA. When the British Merchant Fleet was in full operation, the fishing industry was more or less left to comply with the rules of its own accord, with an occasional random visit by a surveyor when the occasion suited. This was a good working relationship.

There are various opinions on the reasons for the demise of the merchant fleet: the fact that registration in Third World countries with fewer regulations made ships much cheaper to run took many off the British register.

This must have led to a sharp fall in revenue for the Department of Trade and Industry. They suddenly issued a proclamation that fishing vessels of a certain size must come forward for survey, apparently at a cost which was not affordable to many. Very few complied. It was almost impossible to get an Act of Parliament passed on fishing matters in normal times, but overnight a law was passed stating that vessels could not operate without a valid Sea Fishing Safety certificate, issued by a surveyor. There was an option of paying for this by instalments, but failure to comply meant that the vessel was detained, unable to operate and liable to prosecution.

So all registered for a survey, and as long as an initial fee was paid, even if you were behind schedule, you were allowed to operate until a surveyor was available. I found that the first surveyors knew all about merchant ship practice and theory, but very little about fishing boats, shipwright work or commercial fishing. They found themselves in the position of telling professional men, and some of the finest seamen in the world, what they needed, according to a rule-book that was probably conceived by people who had never done the job.

The first Sea Fishing Safety certificates were thus issued not without some differences between surveyors and skippers. But over the years things have become more flexible, and we now have a good working relationship with the present resident surveyor. Some new

The 'Torrey Canyon' wedged firmly on the Seven Stones Reef

regulations were good; others were absurd and conflicted with working practices. There have nevertheless been the usual casualties and loss of lives. It is exasperating when this happens and a politician uses it as an opportunity to make cheap political capital, resulting in more regulations, forcing fishermen to take extra risks just to pay for compliance with them.

Another financial casualty of the shrinkage of the Merchant Fleet was Trinity House, the body responsible for the maintenance of lighthouses and buoys. The revenue of Light Dues paid by merchant ships was reduced considerably, so the cost was passed to the fishing fleet. The lighthouse and buoyage system became obsolete when GPS became accurate to within feet in any weather conditions. However, many navigation points around the UK are maintained in automatic mode and are still serviced, for which we and other boats pay a substantial fee every year.

SEA POLLUTION

The earth's seas are its lifeblood and should be treated with respect. Some people mistake it for a source of infinite capacity to absorb waste, toxic or otherwise. Non-biodegradable materials were the main catch when one of our colleagues fished a small tier of nets in Liverpool Bay. If you hauled that material fifty years hence – millions of plastic bags and holders of all shapes and sizes – except for being covered in green slime, they would look exactly the same.

Such pollution is also a cause of marine accidents. Our engine is fitted with alarms, and the temperature alarm has activated on several occasions just because a plastic bag has been sucked across the cooling water

The Torrey Canyon on the Seven Stones Reef, seeping oil

intake. Having to stop the engine in bad weather and in dangerous waters can be risky. Some fishermen have experienced major engine breakdowns because of half-submerged plastics.

Nobody seems to know the long-term effect of dumping plastics in the sea or on land. Dumping synthetic ropes and nets at sea, most of which float just below the surface, is mindless irresponsibility. We have been towed in on several occasions because a dumped mooring line or net piece has caught in the propeller and stopped the engine, causing damage to the gearbox. One could lose the boat if this happened in dangerous circumstances, threatening lives.

One of the most damaging substances to marine wildlife and beaches is, of course, oil. One morning in 1967, when we mustered to get bait, we learned that the super-tanker *Torrey Canyon* had driven on to the Seven Stones Reef.

It became an international news item and soon the newsmen began to arrive. I was asked to meet the ITN journalist at the Queen's Hotel in Penzance. He greeted me and enquired if I had eaten and 'Would I like a steak?' in an accent straight from the House of Lords.

We agreed on a deal and I was to collect him and his equipment at a specified time from the Scillies. As we approached the islands the Royal Navy was patrolling on the eastern side to keep any traffic away from the reef. This did not present any problems to us, as we knew the navigable channels to the north. This was an interesting variation from fishing – and quite a lark to be dodging the Navy.

We moored in St. Marys, loaded the camera equipment and proceeded to the reef, passing the Navy in a northern channel. As we approached the *Torrey Canyon* the cameraman was wedged in the wheelhouse. We circled the wreck closely several times, getting some of the best clips ever to be filmed throughout the incident.

The heavy ocean swell made the wreck lurch steeply, and all thought that she would slide off the reef and disappear beneath the waves. What a photo scoop that would be! Just at that point the cameraman ran short of film, and I was startled to hear the newsman who was doing the commentaries angrily burst into a stream of language in accent and substance more associated with a fish market than the House of Lords. Despite this, the wreck remained firm.

A loud-hailer from a Navy warship that had spotted us, and which dared not move any closer, drowned everything out with the announcement 'In half an hour a flight of Buccaneers will be here to fire on the wreck.' We made a hasty exit back to the Isles of Scilly and deposited the delighted newsman and his camera equipment, leaving him to join the grandstand view with the Prime Minister, Harold Wilson, and his advisors, and film the remaining proceedings from a high point in the Islands.

We went back to sea and stood well off at a safe distance to watch the fireworks. As the first wave of aircraft veered in a slight westerly breeze was blowing. The first plane lined up for the run; we saw the rockets leave the plane, but the sea breeze carried them wide of the target, and they missed on each successive run.

When the performance was over, the wreck was still un-fired, much to the disappointment of those in the grandstand. Another assault was ordered with different weapons, which eventually did the trick. A billow of black smoke marked the end of the news story. Souvenir hunters appeared everywhere – £100 was even offered for a life-belt. My last view of the *Torrey Canyon* was with a huge bronze propeller, worth thousands of pounds, strapped to her deck. In my lifetime I have seen millions of pounds-worth of flotsam at sea and have never been able to get a penny of it.

The aftermath came with the cleaning of beaches, oil patches on the sea and chemicals for months to come. The oil did not affect the fish, because the South West is open to the Atlantic and there is always a healthy run of fish here. Divers have recently taken an underwater film of the *Torrey Canyon*, showing her covered with weed and becoming a part of the reef.

The fishing port of Grimsby in its heyday
Courtesy of Grimsby & Scunthorpe Newspapers Ltd.

Chapter 7

Politics and Bureaucracy

Politics and bureaucracy have played the major part in the near-extinction of our fishing industry. The beginnings of its demise were the Icelandic Cod Wars, when Iceland, fearing for its fishery from foreign encroachment and catching powers, successively increased its fishing limit, finally to 200 miles.

In spite of a generous quota given to the British distant water boats, this was not acceptable to the administration, which resorted to futile Victorian gunboat diplomacy, sending the Royal Navy within the disputed limits to protect our trawlers.

This resulted in some very odd confrontations. Some of the Icelandic patrol captains, who were previously upheld as heroes for saving the lives of our fishermen by the most heroic acts of bravery in boisterous weather, now found themselves trying to outmanoeuvre the Royal Navy and get into a position from which they could launch a paravane and cut the trawl warps with explosive cutters. This was done in a most gentlemanly and seaman-like manner, as shown on TV's 'Newsnight' – as long as the trawler escaped the same fate.

There was always the possibility that the offending trawler's name would be noted and that at some future date it would be compelled to dock in an Icelandic port

Grimsby, a thriving hive of industry in the mid sixties

Courtesy of Grimsby & Scunthorpe Newspapers Ltd.

by reason of the weather or for a repair, and would then be legally and financially clobbered.

After a time matters were taken to the International Court and the Icelanders, with their powerful political leverage of providing bases for NATO, won the day, and in 1976 the matter was finally settled. Two hundred miles would now be the international sea border limit.

Confidential government papers released under the thirty-year rule uncovered the treachery inherent in the industry's demise – the fishing industry was expendable. As for quota allocation, the UK ended with next to nothing. This sounded the death knell of the distant water fleets. In the major British fishing ports of Grimsby, Hull and Fleetwood the traditional hive of fish marketing, chandlery, engineering and servicing of boats – all trades that had been built up over many generations – began to die, starved of their raw materials. Trawlers now moored nose-to-quay stretched considerable distances.

Jobs were lost. The scrap dealers prospered. Many felt that at some point in the Icelandic dispute a reasonable quota could have been negotiated, and that the Icelanders had a right to control their own fishery. British public opinion was at best lukewarm for its own case. This was a bad day for the British distant water fleet, but the international ruling meant that for the first time in history the UK could claim its own birthright – 200 miles of seaboard area, embracing most of shelf between the Continent with half-way lines.

This area was first recognised by Elizabethan sea dogs as rich fishing grounds. Sir Walter Raleigh was amazed at the varying species. So the near- and middle-water interests awaited an announcement with almost breathless apprehension. Nothing came. During a TV 'Question

Grimsby today – gone are the deep-water trawlers

Time' program the subject was mentioned between a politician and a fisherman. The answer: 'We will secure a superb deal for you. Don't rock the boat, there's a good chap.'

Why couldn't Britain now, as a member country of the EEC, set its own sea limits, for we were told that no sovereignty would be lost on joining the EEC?

When Britain applied to join in 1970, the existing six members realised that the UK would have control of the main fishing grounds if international waters were extended, so immediately inserted a law into the agreement that fish were a common resource – they had tails and could swim anywhere in European waters – to be shared by all in the Common Fisheries Policy.

As we had joined the EEC, we were now in the CFP negotiations between Britain and the EEC over fishery limits. These were battered about for some time – a hundred, fifty and twenty-five miles were speculated.

At this point, the French fisheries minister announced that eighty percent of French fish was caught within fifty miles of the UK coast. The general opinion was that our negotiator was backed into a political corner and had to take what was offered. So a potentially powerful political instrument in the control of our fisheries was signed away. Our negotiator suddenly emerged from the talks proclaiming a superb deal: *six* miles for us and twelve for the Scots, with national quotas of thirty-seven percent for Britain, based on a transitional period ending on December 31st 2002. Fishery critics called it a 'charter of bankruptcy' – which with time is being proved correct.

Spain joined the EEC in 1986 with a fishing fleet bigger than that of any other European state, and the Prime Minister welcomed Spain's entry with the remark that

Fleetwood in its heyday

Maritime Museum of Fleetwood

'The Spanish fishing question has been settled.' A shudder of suspicion went through many in the industry over what had transpired behind closed doors. As Spain had always cast a hungry eye on UK fishing grounds, it added another dimension that in all probability would result in the UK fishing fleet becoming a sacrificial pawn on the chessboard of European politics.

As time passed, Britain signed away in various treaties much of its veto in favour of majority voting, and Spain holds the support of several non-fishery members – plus the political leverage of Gibraltar, which can be used in political persuasion, just as Iceland made use of the presence of US bases. Is it any wonder that the government concedes to almost every Spanish demand, especially when there is any interest in Gibraltar?

To a politician there does not seem to be any mileage in supporting the fishing industry. It poses no threat to their office: fishing constituencies are largely agricultural, business or service-based, make a contribution to the gross national product equivalent to a biscuit factory, and are only suitable for horse-trading. That may or may not be correct at the present, but in the case of Iceland, since it took control of its fisheries, its fishing industry now contributes seventy-five percent of its GNP. In a more recent case, the Faeroes took control of their fisheries and implemented a natural fisheries policy, and has now become one of the richest Atlantic fisheries.

A United Kingdom fishery under similar control would allow the marine environment to re-grow to its normal levels, and fish to spawn in their traditional breeding grounds. This in time would produce a far richer fishery than that of Iceland, which once established would need no cultivation and would more than replenish itself quite

Fleetwood as it is today

naturally. It would produce thousands of real jobs, apart from the wealth and political advantage given by control of access, possibly in the form of licence fees. We have been given a valuable natural gift that is not yet used to its full potential.

Fisheries are seen in the present political climate as a nuisance. When the gross incompetence of the recent Foot and Mouth crisis became known to the public, they shouted for some accountability. The government seized the opportunity to drop 'Agriculture' and 'Fisheries' from the title of the relevant Ministry and for it to be re-named 'DEFRA', the Department for the Environment, Food and Rural Affairs. Was the abolition of fishery and agriculture as industries in mind, when in reality commercial sea fishing should have a specialised ministry of its own, divorced from other departments, as in France?

The political administration, such as it is, is now using DEFRA as a means to extinguish the UK fishing industry into insignificance as part of the grand European strategy. It seems that today's administration does not want a fishing industry that obstructs the political ambitions of Europe. Spain and Portugal are allowed access to the South West fishery, the transitional period has passed, and Brussels has adopted a relentless campaign over the years against the British, so that a third of the remaining fleet has gone through the Multi-Annual Guidance Program (MAGP) to accommodate the Spanish. Looming on the horizon are the Eastern Bloc countries, whose membership has been approved: Poland has a large fishing fleet, which will eventually be entitled to the same fishing rights as other members.

The recent scientific advice that suggested that our traditional cod and chips would be soon be a meal of the

My son, John, with his crew, dumping
fine-quality cod only hours old

past was preceded by an announcement of severe cuts in quotas by the EU, while at the same time allowing industrial trawlers to wipe out the bio feed and anything else in the area, to be processed for animal feed. My son told me recently that he had to dump seventy boxes of good cod in our area for fear of prosecution for being over quota, although he was allowed to land its roe.

These restrictions have put such strains on East Coast and Scottish fishermen that they have made their industry unviable, so some £50 million of decommissioning money was allocated to allow them to leave the industry – as many will, if it is their only choice to avoid bankruptcy. To gain public sympathy, this is done in the name of conservation, but others view it as a ploy to allow room to allocate fishing rights to the Eastern Bloc countries that are about to join the European Union.

Fishermen themselves, some of whose family names have been linked to fishing for centuries, are well aware of conservation issues, and none wish to leave their children the legacy of a barren sea. There is no effective conservation policy in the European Union or the Common Fisheries Policy. Quotas in the mackerel fishery proved unworkable and wasteful, on top of which directives from Brussels that have produced heaps of useless paperwork do more to satisfy political objectives than conservation, with member states showing little political will to abide by any rules.

Quotas were set based on track records. The French inflated theirs considerably, so that when an influx of fine cod suddenly appeared in our coastal waters only a few years ago, our UK quota was soon absorbed by our accurate tracking. As a result, we were compelled to stop landing cod, policed by DEFRA and at pain of large fines, while the rest of our EU partners appeared unrestricted, fishing to capacity.

A similar situation has arisen now. Quotas on pressurised species for any period are set by the EU, supposedly based on scientific advice. Scientists are fine as long as they are able to stick to the truth and to produce accurate facts, uninfluenced by their employers. But equally important is the experienced fisherman, who has had to earn a living for himself, his crew and to keep his boat viable. Neither could do the other's jobs, but both contribute from their respective mines of information. Nevertheless, the experienced fisherman does not appear to influence any formulation of fishing policy.

Chapter 8

Changes in Fishing over the Years

I have often been asked by the press and television what differences exist between now and when I entered the industry, some forty-five years ago.

In those days there was a body called the White Fish Authority that provided public assistance to bona fide fishermen in the form of financial grants and loans for things like new boats, engines and gear, and many benefited from this.

Later, after joining the EEC, the White Fish Authority was superseded by the Sea Fish Industry Authority, which performed the same function. It soon became apparent that there were too many boats, armed with all the latest technology, chasing too few fish. So the first step was to issue licences: it is only fair to mention that this is internationally adopted to control the catching effort, particularly by countries with limited fisheries, where a licence is worth more than the boat and can be obtained only by the loss of another boat from the existing fleet.

In the EU the licensing scheme the affects the UK, the annual Total Allowable Catch (TAC) for the member states, is set by Brussels based on scientific advice. The TAC is divided between the member states, and the UK quota is divided between the producer organisation memberships, with some going to non-producer organisation members.

The producer organisation can lease or buy quotas from vessels that have left the industry or are not fishing for a particular species. Each vessel is given a quota of species, which is specified in writing on its licence. If the boat exceeds that quota, its owner is compelled to buy or lease additional quote from producer organisations, or from anyone else with available quota.

To remain within the law, a vessel can also buy or lease quota on the assumption that it will be needed at some future date. If a vessel buys quota those units are added to its annual quota and are ring-fenced permanently to its licence. This constitutes a gamble on the future of the industry, because if Brussels decides on an increase or decrease in quota, the value of purchased quota units can rise or fall.

At present anyone wishing to enter the industry, starting from zero, must realise that they will not receive any financial assistance from public bodies for boats, engines, electronics, gear and so on, and will also need to purchase a licence with a proven track record.

A considerable amount of money is therefore required, as the present rate for buying leases varies according to species. With a hake lease costing £700 per ton and the purchase of the quota costing £3,500 per ton, should the auction price for hake fall, it could mean that the fish had been caught for almost nothing at all.

But the most frustrating part is the number of DEFRA officials whose area administrators apply the EU fishing regulations to the letter, seeking to prove in law that prime fish that should have been dumped was actually marketed. Fishermen being forced to dump tons of prime fish – which might be legally right, but is certainly morally wrong – is threatening bankruptcy to many if found guilty, and is also threatening the existence of Newlyn as one of the last major UK fishing ports.

The principal cause for obstructing a livelihood in commercial fishing used to be bad weather, but DEFRA officials seem to have overtaken the elements.

Our boat, along with a dozen others, is currently under investigation for alleged log-book offences, and other fishermen might be concerned about falling into the same legal pothole. In my early days, MAFF always had an amicable and supportive relationship with the fishing industry, with few offences. This relationship now seems to have changed, with some DEFRA officials being regarded as the 'secret police', while the area administration is likened by some to Reinhard Heydrich's treatment of the Czech, prosecuting fifty-eight different offences and imposing fines ranging from five to fifty thousand pounds.

I recently received a radio message from my son, who was nearing the end of a seven-day trip at sea and a hundred miles out in bad weather. He had caught one and a half tons of cod over quota and he enquired whether DEFRA would allow him to auction it off for charity. The reply came back 'That is not allowed.' Having once been fined £3,000 for doing virtually nothing, it does not take much imagination to guess what the size of the fine would be for landing over quota. There was, therefore, no option left but to dump a ton and a half of prime cod. Our gear only catches fully-matured fish, so every one of those dumped fish is at least four, and up to ten years old!

Most of the other gill netters in Newlyn are in the same predicament: whichever area is fished, cod is caught and dumped. This makes a nonsense of the

Newlyn 2003 – a busy fishing port

Original painting by Jeffrey E. Lawrence

directive issued by Brussels concerning the restrictive cod quota for all sea areas, which is fed to the public in the name of conservation.

Yesterday was the first day of Spring 2003, and never in my whole life of commercial fishing have I seen the industry at such a low ebb. One sees the industry as the vanguard that foreshadows the fate of a country steeped in a mire of bureaucracy from endless streams of directives issued by Brussels, many of which seem to be designed to give a commercial advantage to our EU partners.

These go straight into English law, spawning a small army of jumped-up officials, leading to considerable expansion of the original directives and resulting in increased costs all round. This not only affects fishing, but also has a more widespread impact, so that, for example, small businesses and old people's homes are forced to close.

Napoleon said *'L'Angleterre est une nation de boutiquiers'* – that England was 'a nation of shopkeepers', and De Gaulle commented on our application to join the EEC that 'England, in effect, is insular. She is maritime... England's structure, England's very situation differs profoundly from those of the Continentals.' Nelson was in praise of fishermen for their maritime contribution as a source of sea-faring expertise, but in these days of modern weapons that appears to be irrelevant.

Our troubles began with the signing of the Treaty of Rome, when the British electorate, including me, voted 'Yes' on the referendum on assurance from the politicians that we were joining collective free-trading states and that no sovereignty would be lost. We now realise that we were deceived by lies and half-truths and that most of

The annual Newlyn Fish Festival.
Is it going to suffer the fate of Grimsby?

our country's present ills can be traced directly or indirectly to EU law and directives.

The Continental style of Mafia politics has permeated to our own politicians, who in pre-war days held their positions with the honourable slogan 'Country first, party second, self last.' This now seems to work in the reverse order, and they are viewed by many as incompetent, unaccountable and unprincipled opportunists, riding the gravy train of Brussels and Westminster with inflated expense accounts. We are in almost as perilous a political position as in 1940, just with the military dimension removed from the equation. All the main political parties have at some time contributed to the present situation in which open political debate appears to be taboo, anaesthetising the electorate into apathy. My shipmates lying in a watery grave would ask 'Did we give our lives for the extinction of democracy?'

It is interesting to note that there are few net contributions into the EEC, particularly from the new batch of recruits from the Eastern Bloc. Most members receive more in grants than they contribute, and the last trading figures I saw showed a huge deficit with the EU since we joined. Are these the basic lines on which to run a state that at some point in time must face a crisis? A business run under similar lines would face bankruptcy.

It would take a politician of Churchillian calibre to extricate us from the mire of corruption, fraud, sleaze and waste called the EU, in which the chief auditor can only account for five percent of budget. Our own contribution to this exclusive club is £3 billion net per year, for which I can see no benefits. I fail to understand how closer links with the EU, drawing us piecemeal into the black hole of one federal state, will not demonstrate the glaring history lessons of Yugoslavia and the Soviet Union – that you cannot weld together established and different cultures and languages into one entity.

Leaving the EU would give us the opportunity to reclaim our country, our birthright and our fishing industry – which would be accountable under our own laws, as are those of Iceland, Norway and Greenland. Once managed properly, with fishermen also taking an active role, the fishing industry would quickly replenish itself and, as long as the ocean currents remained in their prescribed paths and the Gulf Stream survived the effects of global warming, would give politicians powerful influence over access rights.

I am now in my twilight years but still hope to see this come to pass, mainly for the sake of the country, but also for that of future generations of fishermen. Failure would eventually leave us a vanquished nation, dominated by a Franco-German axis and subordinate to the EU, with the centre of world finance moved from London to Frankfurt, stripped of our gold reserves, oil and...

...fishing gone.

Acknowledgements

The author would like to thank the following people and organisations.

For their kindness in granting permission for their illustrations to be used in this book:

The Imperial War Museum, London:

Page 6, negative no. A27579

Page 8, negative no. FL1300

Page 10, negative no. C2647

Page 12, top, negative no. A20973

Page 12, top, negative no. NA176

Page 16, negative no. ZZZ1811C

Page 18, negative no. MISC51235

Page 20, top, negative no. MH4681

Page 20, bottom, negative no. MISC51236

Page 22, top, negative no. A9419

Page 22, bottom, negative no. A22031

Page 24, negative no. A31001

Page 26, negative no. CA122

Page 28, negative no. ZZZ207013

Page 30, negative no. CH1354

Morrab Library, Penzance:

Page 76, top, ref. RWG/12/11

Page 76, bottom, ref. WG/12/1

Page 86, ref. RCG/12/106

Page 88, top, ref. RHG/12/18

Page 88, bottom, ref. RHG/12/13

Page 108, ref. Angove wreck 8.023

Page 110, ref. 8.023

Grimsby & Scunthorpe Newspapers Ltd:

Page 114

Page 116

Richard Major:

Page 50 and rear cover

Page 52

Page 82

Page 84

The Maritime Museum of Fleetwood: page 120

Jeffrey E. Lawrence, Newlyn: page 130, original painting.

Anne Woodhams, for assistance with initial digitisation and proofing of manuscript.

The photograph of the *Rarau* on page 80 is Crown Copyright/MOD and is reproduced with the permission of Her Majesty's Stationary Office.